D0813546

NEW CRITICISM *Series*
no. 1

First MIT Press edition, 1989

Cover:
Jaen Anderson

Painting:
Masterpieces (Warhol) 1986 by Maria Kozic, acrylic on wood

Printed in Italy
Novastampa, Parma
February 1989

Copyright 1989
Giancarlo Politi Editore
799 Broadway, Rm. 237, New York, NY 10003

Library of Congress Catalog
Card no. 88-62705

ISBN 0-262-70037-9

P A U L   T A Y L O R

POST-POP ART

Flash Art
BOOKS

The MIT Press
Cambridge, Massachusetts

ACKNOWLEDGEMENTS

"Detournement As Negation and Prelude" from *International Situationniste* magazine, number 3, Paris 1959. Reprinted from *Situationist International Anthology*, edited and translated by Ken Knabb, Berkeley, Bureau of Public Secrets, 1981. "In Poor Taste" from *Block* magazine, number 8, London, 1983. Reprinted by kind permission of the author. "That Old Thing, Art..." from the catalogue of the exhibition *Pop Art* at the Palazzo Grassi, Venice, first published by Electa, 1980; in France in the collection, *L'obvie et l'obtus,* Editions du Seuil, Paris 1982; and in the current translation by Richard Howard in *The Responsibility of Forms.* Translation © 1985 by Farrar, Straus and Giroux, Inc., New York. Reprinted by permission of Hill and Wang, a division of Farrar, Straus and Giroux, Inc. "Pop: An Art of Consumption" from *La société de consommation: ses mythes, ses structures,* Paris, Gallimard, 1970. For this translation and suggestions for the re-translation of "Beyond the Vanishing Point of Art" delivered as a lecture at the Whitney Museum of American Art, New York, I am grateful to Paul Foss, editor, *Art & Text,* Melbourne. "The Cultural Politics of Pop" from *New German Critique*, number 4, 1975, Milwaukee and *After the Great Divide.* Reprinted here by kind permission of the author and Indiana University Press © 1985. "Punk: Political Pop" from the L.A.I.C.A. *Journal,* Los Angeles 1979. Reprinted by kind permission of the author. Anthology and Introduction © 1989 Paul Taylor.

Contents

DETOURNEMENT AS NEGATION AND PRELUDE
G U Y   D E B O R D

Detournement, the re-use of pre-existing artistic elements in a new ensemble, has been a constantly present tendency of the contemporary avant-garde both before and since the establishment of the Situationist International. The two fundamental laws of detournement are the loss of importance of each detourned autonomous element—which may go so far as to lose its original sense completely—and at the same time the organization of another meaningful ensemble that confers on each element its new scope and effect.

Detournement has a peculiar power which obviously stems from the double meaning, from the enrichment of most of the terms by the coexistence within them of their old senses and their new, immediate senses. Detournement is practical because it is so easy to use and because of its inexhaustible potential for re-use. Concerning the negligible effort required for detournement, we have already said, "The cheapness of its products is the heavy artillery that breaks through all the Chinese walls of understanding," (*Methods of Detournement*, May 1956). But these points would not by themselves justify recourse to this method, which the same text describes as

"clashing head-on against all social and legal conventions."
Detournement has a historical significance. What is it?

"Detournement is a game made possible by the capacity of *devaluation*," writes Jorn in his study *Detourned Painting* (May 1959), and he goes on to say that all the elements of the cultural past must be "reinvested" or disappear. Detournement is thus first of all a negation of the value of the previous organization of expression. It arises and grows increasingly stronger in the historical period of the decomposition of artistic expression. But at the same time, the attempts to reuse the "detournable bloc" as material for other ensembles express the search for a vaster construction, a new genre of creation at a higher level.

The SI is a very special kind of movement, of a nature different from preceding artistic avant-gardes. Within culture the SI can be likened to a research laboratory, for example, or to a party in which we are situationists but nothing that we do is situationist. This is not a disavowal for anyone. We are partisans of a certain future of culture, of life. Situationist activity is a definite craft which we are not yet practicing.

Thus the signature of the situationist movement, the sign of its presence and contestation in contemporary cultural reality (since we cannot represent any common style whatsoever), is first of all the use of detournement. We may mention, on the level of detourned expression, Jorn's altered paintings; Debord and Jorn's book *Mémoires*, "composed entirely of prefabricated elements," in which the writing on each page runs in all directions and the reciprocal relations of the phrases are invariably uncompleted; Constant's projects for detourned sculptures; and Debord's detourned documen-

8

tary film, *On the Passage of a Few Persons Through a Rather Brief Period of Time*. On the level of what *Methods of Detournement* calls "ultra-detournement, that is, the tendencies for detournement to operate in everyday social life" (e.g. passwords or the wearing of disguises, belonging to the sphere of play) we might mention, at different levels, Gallizio's industrial painting; Wyckaert's "orchestral" project for assembly-line painting with a division of labor based on color; and numerous detournements of buildings that were at the origin of unitary urbanism. But we should also mention in this context the SI's very forms of "organization" and propaganda.

At this point in the world's development all forms of expression are losing all grip on reality and being reduced to self-parody. As the readers of this journal can frequently verify, present-day writing always has an element of parody. "It is necessary," states *Methods of Detournement*, "to conceive of a parodic-serious stage where the accumulation of detourned elements, far from aiming at arousing indignation or laughter by alluding to some original work, will express our indifference toward a meaningless and forgotten original, and concern itself with rendering a certain sublimity."

The parodic-serious expresses the contradictions of an era in which we find ourselves confronted with both the urgent necessity and the near impossibility of bringing together and carrying out a totally innovative collective action. An era in which the greatest seriousness advances masked in the ambiguous interplay between art and its negation; in which the essential voyages of discovery have been undertaken by such astonishingly incapable people.

INTRODUCTION
PAUL TAYLOR

Two and a half decades after the event, Pop Art has re-emerged as the most influential movement in the contemporary art world. Alive and mutating, it entered yet another new phase in 1987 with the death of Andy Warhol. Warhol's famous and shocking death was a journalistic event, a new idea in the world of American publishing. As was to be expected, it has given rise to a publishing and exhibition boom that comprises Warhol museum retrospectives, photograph albums, biographies, memoirs and re-issues of the artist's early publications. Yet it is also proving to be of museographic importance because Andy Warhol is the first major American artist of the 1960s, indeed the first of the entire post-Abstract Expressionist generation in America, to pass into history. Now, traditional museum blockbuster survey exhibitions that scan the march of art over the centuries can take a step closer to the present by adding his art to their roster. In this sense, Warhol has become the newest modern artist, and Pop Art has become newly poised for assimilation into art history's grand procession.

Andy Warhol, of course, has already been back on the art

world's mind for some time. He not only typified Pop Art, but was also the artist who most conspicuously lived out the things that Pop represented. Warhol the man simulated the specialness of the things depicted in his art, transforming himself from a hungry artist who paints a sumptuous meal to the very image of its attainment and consumption. He built a space around himself that was an exact photocopy of the isolation of the objects in his paintings. It is this kind of space, this unnatural distance from other things and people, this fame, that for many subsequent artists has become the measure of success. In the wake of Warhol, removal from the world has become art's reward.

Yet Andy Warhol's influence is more insidious still. His repetitive image paintings, such as his multiple soup can paintings of 1962, are wholly original in the canon of modern painting. Their repeated use of borrowed material in a manner that absented the hand of the artist cannot be considered outside of today's preoccupation with theories of authorship. Moreover, his repeated single images predate the repetition of identical elements in the sculpture of the Minimal artists. Formally, their only precedent was the grid-like pictorial designs that are an *idée fixe* of Modernism. Warhol's pictures do combine ideas from the art of Jasper Johns and Robert Rauschenberg: Johns's earlier alphabet paintings feature repeated motifs, (though these motifs are different from one another), and Rauschenberg's silkscreened paintings have repeated images, though they never occupy the entire space. Yet the serial arrangement of Warhol's images, which invites the viewer to "read" the surface in the manner of a page and also to "see" it as a pattern, was new.

According to Roland Barthes, serialism introduced the element of time into painting. Time is also the issue in a consideration of the current Pop Art revival. Pop was initially a challenge to the historicist process, to the idea of the natural supercession of styles in art. It was a questioning of the concept of the new in art history. Somehow, Pop now seems exempt from the process of conventional art history whereby art movements are sealed off, finished and relegated to the past once something new has come along—perhaps because Pop already used second-hand images, because "invention" was not an issue. Pop's relevance to artists and critics today, its sheer persistence, shows up the contemporary art world's reluctance to invent new forms and willingness instead to celebrate the recycling of the past. To some, this is profoundly unsettling. The 1980s revival of Pop may be interpreted as proof of the fatal repetitiveness of art—of art, that is, since Pop.

Pop Art has always had its detractors, cultural and art critics of the left and right alike who are united in regarding Pop as a reactionary by product of the advanced industrial society and see Pop Art's renewed influence on art as an indication of art's decadence in the grip of either the art market or political ideology. And of course Pop's morbid fascination with consumer goods, mass-culture, publicity and mechanical reproduction has also appalled those for whom art should embody nobler, less commercial values. Indeed in 1989, Pop Art's "new novelty"—the new art historical and commercial mileage that it is bestowing on museums, publishing houses and the like since Warhol's death—is making Pop Art's relationship with the culture industry even more official and entrenched, and Pop Art an even more commercially viable movement. The notion of it as a subversive and critical creative activity is, to some, less conceivable now than ever. Yet, the creative and critical potential of Pop is precisely what the essays in this anthology argue.

As is to be expected, most of the existing literature on Pop Art was published in the 1960s. Of the following essays, the earliest is from 1970, by which time Pop was roundly considered "over." At the end of the '60s, the Minimalist, Postminimalist and Conceptual art movements had hit the covers of the international art journals, and while Pop Art had found a ready audience among both art collectors and consumers of the mass media for whom it signified the ultimate intersection of historical and fashionable style, serious art critics had turned to new issues. Eventually, Pop Art became a non-issue. For some, the art of Roy Lichtenstein, James Rosenquist, Claes Oldenburg, Warhol and others was merely the first of the novelty art movements. To many critics, the most interesting aspect of Pop was sociological. Its effects were temporary and irrelevant to subsequent artistic developments. Others insisted that Pop Art's flirtation with advertising and publicity was a genuine, not merely an ironic, acquiescence to the power of the dominant culture and its media. And still others went no further than to establish Pop's rightful claim as art. The usefulness of all these positions is not disputed in this anthology; other things are at stake.

Work on this anthology of translations and new essays about Pop art was started in 1986, before the current boom. The reasons for compiling it were, therefore, unrelated to the nostalgia for Warhol, although the essays do share a new regard for Pop Art in general, and for Andy Warhol in particular. This new attitude about Pop Art is partly due to the cultural and political biases shared by the essayists. Each of the essays, from Jean Baudrillard's 1970 text (where his debt to Situationism is clear) to the three essays—by Baudrillard, David Deitcher and Mary Anne Staniszewski—that were written after Warhol's death, makes a case for the oppositional, culturally provocative aspects of Pop Art. That critics can still find in Pop a model for political debate is only one of the multitude of paradoxes that abound in this seemingly most impassive and celebratory of art movements.

A roughly common understanding of the role of culture, especially of avant-garde art in the era of its mass appeal, forms the background to these texts. Even the essays that demonstrate the exaggerated commodity status of Pop Art are at pains to demonstrate that it offers a penetrating critique of cultural consumption. Far from being a simple artistic echo of the advertising and merchandising worlds, Pop Art is one of the most extreme perspectives from which we can critically reflect on them. Shot through by irony and an ambivalent, parasitical relation to the art marketplace, Pop was an original test case of art's function in a post-Romantic age. It addressed a sophisticated audience for whom the mythic idea of the artist as an heroic individual had matured into an idea of artist as a celebrity.

All of these essays are manifestly secondary texts, based on the well-known primary sources: original exhibition catalogues, magazine articles, interviews, and classic Pop Art textbooks of the 1960s. The initial critics of Pop Art, its champions and detractors alike, are largely absent from this collection. However, at a distance of years (and, in some cases, kilometres) from Pop Art's original impulses, writers such as Barthes (in one of his last essays, from 1980) did not believe that the shock of Pop was lessened by time and place.

Pop's emergence in Britain was radically different from its development in New York, yet the subject-matter was universally American. (Its blatant Americanness was only later edited out of Pop Art, as in the painting of the German artists Sigmar Polke and Gerhard Richter). However, as with the Punk rock movement of the 1970s, discussed here briefly by Dick Hebdige and at length by Dan Graham, Pop Art emerged out of a curious, transatlantic dialectic. The Punk and New Wave music, art and fashion nexus originated in New York in the early and mid-70s as a delayed reaction to the multidisciplinary Pop scene most famously acted out in Warhol's "Factory" of the previous decade. Yet Punk reached its most sensational, even "classic," manifestations in the late '70s in London. Similarly, Pop's revolt against so-called High Modernism which is conventionally understood to have evolved from the art of the New York School in the usual manner of stylistic cause and effect was independently articulated in many of the French Situationist texts and in the art and design activities of young British artists and critics of the 1950s.

British Pop artists and critics have suggested that their movement was in many ways a reaction to the influx of post-war American household commodities and advertising. Incorporating images of objects of collective societal desire into their collages and paintings (everything from consumer goods to Pop stars was grist for the mill) and copying the slick look of machine fabrication was for British Pop artists a quick and efficient way of appropriating the powerful attraction of

16

mass-produced images. Yet both British and American Pop Art were manifestations of envy. Pop Art's strongest impulse was to steal. Andy Warhol (whose book, *The Philosophy of Andy Warhol: From A to B and Back Again*, 1975, features a whole chapter about jealousy) expressed a longing, in turn, for the Swinging Sixties in London, and his "Factory" was initially a provincial copy of the more glamorous and hip English scene. It was especially Warhol's dandyish pose, as is recounted in Andreas Huyssen's essay on Pop's "politics," that spread around the world. Outside the United States, where it was perceived as a criticism of American capitalism, Pop Art was a resounding influence and success in Europe, and in Germany in particular. It afforded a startling opportunity to reflect on the differences between post-war America and the spread of a multinational culture.

The European Situationist writers attacked Pop Art. Earlier, however, they had advocated an art like Pop (based on Dada and Surrealist examples) that drew from non-art media, including comics, newspapers and the movies, with a revolutionary wish to dissolve and redistribute art into everyday life. Then, when the commercial Pop Art movement appeared in the 1960s, they dismissed it. Despite the judgement of such important precursors, the Pop artists, especially Andy Warhol, did play a significant role in the process by which the category of high art was destroyed and the character of the avant-garde artist transformed from that of a specialist into an amateur. Warhol integrated the fine and commercial arts, and promoted the possibility of the modern artist as an artistically radical entrepreneur.

Pop Art went underground until the mid-1970s, when it

re-emerged in London's self-consciously artistic Punk scene. As Warhol argued in his book, *POPism: The Warhol Sixties* (1980), the resemblances between the New Wave scene and the Warhol days at the Factory were considerable. While Warhol's account focuses on his own subterranean milieu, the similarities between Pop Art and New Wave music, graphics and fashion can easily be found in the material, style and imagery of the work of both movements. Artistic quotation of distant sources that arrive in one's own place through the media continues to characterize art today, "post-Pop." (The paintings of the British artist Simon Linke which directly copy the advertisement pages of an American art magazine are only the latest manifestations of this ongoing, intercontinental reciprocation).

Pop Art's characteristic devices of artistic quotation or appropriation and incorporation of low-art materials re-emerged among a whole new generation at the end of the 1970s for whom the prospects of reworking second-hand imagery were immense. This "second career" of Pop Art is doubtessly due to the emergence of artists such as Cindy Sherman, David Salle, Sherrie Levine and Kenny Scharf in New York and lesser known artists everywhere in the last ten years who recognized that Pop was predicated on a similar kind of vicarious pleasure, voyeuristic detachment from its objects, and materialistic envy of the unattainable as that which characterized their own taste.

Hence repetition, which characterizes Warhol's method, also characterizes his influence. Pop Art heralded a whole culture of repetition, a society that shamelessly entertains itself by repeating itself. In our present utopia of inauthenticity, the production of originals is increasingly scarce, although the production of art has multiplied. It is at least appropriate, therefore, that this anthology's attempt to provoke original ways of reconsidering Pop should take the form of a book made up from pre-existing materials.

THAT OLD THING, ART . . .
ROLAND BARTHES

As all the encyclopedias remind us, during the fifties certain artists at the London Institute of Contemporary Arts became advocates of the popular culture of the period: comic strips, films, advertising, science fiction, pop music. These various manifestations did not derive from what is generally called an Aesthetic but were entirely produced by Mass Culture and did not participate in art at all; simply, certain artists, architects, and writers were interested in them. Crossing the Atlantic, these products forced the barrier of art; accommodated by certain American artists, they became works of art, of which culture no longer constituted the being, merely the reference: origin was displaced by citation. Pop Art as we know it is the permanent theater of this tension: on one hand, the mass culture of the period is present in it as a revolutionary force which contests art; and on the other, art is present in it as a very old force which irresistibly returns in the economy of societies. There are two voices, as in a fugue—one says: "This is not Art"; the other says, at the same time: "I am Art."

Art is something which must be destroyed—a proposition common to many experiments of Modernity.

Pop Art reverses values. "What characterizes Pop is mainly its use of what is despised" (Lichtenstein). Images from mass culture, regarded as vulgar, unworthy of an aesthetic consecration, return virtually unaltered as materials of the artist's activity. I should like to call this reversal the "Clovis Complex": like Saint Remi addressing the Frankish king, the god of Pop Art says to the artist: "Burn what you have worshipped, worship what you have burned." For instance: photography has long been fascinated by painting, of which it still passes as a poor relation; Pop Art overturns this prejudice: the photograph often becomes the origin of the images Pop Art presents: neither "art painting" nor "art photograph," but a nameless mixture. Another example of reversal: nothing more contrary to art than the notion of being the mere reflection of the things represented; even photography does not support this destiny; Pop Art, on the contrary, accepts being an *imagery*, a collection of reflections, constituted by the banal reverberation of the American environment: reviled by high art, the copy returns. This reversal is not capricious, it does not proceed from a simple denial of value, from a simple rejection of the past; it obeys a regular historical impulse; as Paul Valéry noted (in *Pièces sur l'Art*), the appearance of new technical means (here, photography, serigraphy) modifies not only art's forms but its very concept.

Repetition is a feature of culture. I mean that we can make use of repetition in order to propose a certain typology of cultures. Popular or extra-European cultures (deriving from an ethnography) acknowledge as much, and derive meaning and pleasure from the fact (we need merely instance today's minimal music and disco); Occidental high culture does not (even if it has resorted to repetition more than we suppose, in the baroque period). Pop Art, on the other hand, repeats—spectacularly. Warhol proposes a series of identical images *(White Burning Car Twice)* or of images which differ only by some slight variation of color *(Flowers, Marilyn)*. The stake of these repetitions (or of Repetition as a method) is not only the destruction of art but also (moreover, they go together) another conception of the human subject: repetition affords access, in effect, to a different temporality: where the Occidental subject experiences the ingratitude of a world from which the New—i.e., ultimately, Adventure—is excluded, the Warholian subject (since Warhol is a practitioner of these repetitions) abolishes the pathos of time in himself, because this pathos is always linked to the feeling that something has appeared, will die, and that one's death is opposed only by being transformed into a second something which does not resemble the first. For Pop Art, it is important that things be "finite" (outlined: no evanescence), but it is not important that they be finished, that work (is there a work?) be given the internal organization of a destiny (birth, life, death). Hence we must unlearn the boredom of the "endless" (one of Warhol's first films, ★ ★ ★ ★, lasted twenty-five hours; *Chelsea Girls* lasts three and a half). Repetition disturbs the person (that classical entity) in another fashion: by multiplying the same image, Pop Art rediscovers the theme of the Double, of the Doppelgänger; this is a mythic theme (the Shadow, the Man or the Woman without a Shadow); but in the productions of Pop Art, the Double is harmless—has lost all maleficent or moral power, neither threatens nor haunts: the Double is a Copy, not a Shadow: *beside,* not *behind:* a flat, insignificant, hence irreligious Double.

Repetition of the portrait induces an adulteration of the person (a notion simultaneously civic, moral, psychological, and of course historical). Pop Art, it has also been said, takes the place of a machine; it prefers to utilize mechanical processes of reproduction: for example, it freezes the star (Marilyn, Liz) in her image *as star:* no more soul, nothing but a strictly imaginary status, since the star's being is the icon. The object itself, which in everyday life we incessantly personalize by incorporating into our individual world—the object is, according to Pop Art, no longer anything but the residue of a subtraction: everything left over from a tin can once we have mentally amputated all its possible themes, all its possible uses. Pop Art is well aware that the fundamental expression of the person is style. As Buffon said (a celebrated remark, once known to every French schoolboy): "Style is the man." Take away style and there is no longer any (individual) man. The notion of style, in all the arts, has therefore been linked, historically, to a humanism of the person. Consider an unlikely example, that of "graphism": manual writing, long impersonal (during Antiquity and the Middle Ages), began to be individualized in the Renaissance, dawn of the modern period; but today, when the person is a moribund idea, or at least a menaced one, under the pressure of the gregarious forces which animate mass culture, the personality of writing is fading art. There is, as I see it, a certain relation between Pop Art and what is called "script," that anonymous writing sometimes taught to dysgraphic children because it is inspired by the neutral and, so to speak, elementary features of typography. Further, we must realize that if Pop Art depersonalizes, it does not make anonymous: nothing is more identifiable than Marilyn, the electric chair, a telegram, or a dress, as seen by Pop Art; they are in fact *nothing but that:* immediately and exhaustively identifiable, thereby teaching us that identity is not the person: the future world risks being a world of identities (by the computerized proliferation of police files), but not of persons.

A final feature which attaches Pop Art to the experiments of Modernity: the banal conformity of representation to the thing represented. "I don't want a canvas," Rauschenberg says, "to look like what it isn't. I want it to look like what it is." The proposition is aggressive in that art has always regarded itself as an inevitable detour that must be taken in order to "render" the truth of the thing. What Pop Art wants is to desymbolize the object, to give it the obtuse and matte stubbornness of a fact (John Cage: "The object is a fact, not a symbol"). To say the object is asymbolic is to deny it possesses a profound or proximate space through which its appearance can propagate vibrations of meaning: Pop Art's object (this is a true revolution of language) is neither metaphoric nor metonymic; it presents itself cut off from its source and its

25

surroundings; in particular, the Pop artist does not stand *behind* his work, and he himself has no depth: he is merely the surface of his pictures: no signified, no intention, anywhere. Now the fact, in mass culture, is no longer an element of the natural world; what appears as fact is the stereotype: what everyone sees and consumes. Pop Art finds the unity of its representations in the radical conjunction of these two forms, each carried to extremes: the stereotype and the image. Tahiti is a fact, insofar as a unanimous and persistent public opinion designates this site as a collection of palm trees, of flowers worn over one ear, of long hair, sarongs, and languorous, enticing glances (Lichtenstein's *Little Aloha*). In this way, Pop Art produces certain *radical images*: by dint of being an image, the thing is stripped of any symbol. This is an audacious movement of mind (or of society): it is no longer the fact which is transformed into an image (which is, strictly speaking, the movement of metaphor, out of which humanity has made poetry for centuries), it is the image which becomes a fact. Pop Art thus features a philosophical quality of things, which we may call *facticity*: the *factitious* is the character of what exists as fact and appears stripped of any justification: not only are the objects represented by Pop Art factitious, but they incarnate the very concept of facticity—that by which, in spite of themselves, they begin to signify again: they signify that they signify nothing.

For meaning is cunning: drive it away and it gallops back. Pop Art seeks to destroy art (or at least to do without it), but art rejoins it: art is the counter-subject of our fugue.

The attempt has been made to abolish the signified, and thereby the sign; but the signifier subsists, persists, even if it does not refer, apparently, to anything. What is the signifier? Let us say, to be quick about it: the thing perceived, augmented by a certain thought. Now, in Pop Art, this supplement exists—as it exists in all the world's arts.

First of all, quite frequently, Pop Art changes the level of our perception; it diminishes, enlarges, withdraws, advances, extends the multiplied object to the dimensions of a signboard, or magnifies it as if it were seen under a jeweler's *loupe*. Now, once proportions are changed, art appears (it suffices to think of architecture, which is an art of *the size of things*): it is not by accident that Lichtenstein reproduces a *loupe* and what it enlarges: *Magnifying Glass* is in a sense the emblem of Pop Art.

And then, in many works of Pop Art, the background against which the object is silhouetted, or even out of which it is made, has a powerful existence (rather of the kind clouds had in classical painting): there is an importance of the grid. This comes, perhaps, from Warhol's first experiments: serigraphs depend on textile (textile and grid are the same thing); it is as if our latest modernity enjoys this manifestation of the grid, at once consecrating the raw material (grain of the paper in Twombly's work) and the mechanization of reproduction (micro-pattern of the computer portraits). Grid is a kind of obsession (a thematics, criticism would have said not long ago); it participates in various exchanges; its perceptual role is inverted (in Lichtenstein's aquarium, water consists of polka dots); it is enlarged in a deliberately infantile fashion (Lichtenstein's sponge consists of holes, like a piece

27

of Gruyère); the mechanical texture is exemplarily imitated (again, Lichtenstein's *Large Spool*). Here art appears in the emphasis on what should be insignificant.

Another emphasis (and consequently another return of art): color. Of course, everything found in nature and *a fortiori* in the social world is colored; but if it is to remain a factitious object, as a true destruction of art would have it, its color itself must remain *indeterminate*. Now, this is not the case: Pop Art's colors are intentional and, we might even say (a real denial), subject to a *style*: they are intentional first of all because they are always the same ones and hence have a thematic value; then because this theme has a value as meaning: Pop color is openly chemical; it aggressively refers to the artifice of chemistry, in its opposition to Nature. And if we admit that, in the plastic domain, color is ordinarily the site of pulsion, these acrylics, these flat primaries, these lacquers, in short these colors which are never shades, since nuance is banished from them, seek to cut short desire, emotion: we might say, at the limit, that they have a moral meaning, or at least that they systematically rely on a certain frustration. Color and even substance (lacquer, plaster) give Pop Art a meaning and consequently make it an art; we will be convinced of this by noticing that Pop artists readily define their canvases by the color of the objects represented: *Black Girl, Blue Wall, Red Door* (Segal), *Two Blackish Robes* (Dine).

Pop is an art because, just when it seems to renounce all meaning, consenting only to reproduce things in their platitude, it stages, according to certain methods proper to it and forming a style, an object which is neither the thing nor its meaning, but which is: its signifier, or rather: the Signifier. Art—any art, from poetry to comic strips—exists the moment our glance has the Signifier as its object. Of course, in the productions of art, there is usually a signified (here, mass culture), but this signified, finally, appears in an *indirect* position: obliquely, one might say; so true is it that meaning, the play of meaning, its abolition, its return, is never anything but a *question of place*. Moreover, it is not only because the Pop artist stages the Signifier that his work derives from and relates to art; it is also because this work is *looked at* (and not only seen); however much Pop Art has depersonalized the world, platitudinized objects, dehumanized images, replaced traditional craftsmanship of the canvas by machinery, some "subject" remains. What subject? The one who looks, in the absence of the one who makes. We can fabricate a machine, but someone who looks at it is not a machine—he desires, he fears, he delights, he is bored, etc. This is what happens with Pop Art.

I add: Pop is an art of the essence of things, it is an "ontological" art. Look how Warhol proceeds with his repetitions—initially conceived as a method meant to destroy art: he repeats the image so as to suggest that the object trembles before the lens or the gaze; and if it trembles, one might say, it is because it seeks itself: it seeks its essence, it seeks to put this essence before you; in other words, the trembling of the thing acts (this is its effect-as-meaning) as a pose: in the past, was not the pose—before the easel or the lens—the affirmation of an individual's essence? Marilyn, Liz, Elvis, Troy Donahue are not presented, strictly speaking, according to their contingency, but according to their eternal identity: they have an "eidos," which it is the task of Pop Art to represent. Now look at Lichtenstein: he does not repeat, but his task is the same: he reduces, he purifies the image in order to intercept (and offer) what? its rhetorical essence: here art's entire labor consists not, as in the past, in streamlining the stylistic artifices of discourse, but on the contrary, in cleansing the image of everything in it which is not rhetoric: what must be expelled, like a vital nucleus, is the code essence. The philosophical meaning of this labor is that modern things have no essence other than the social code which manifests them—so that ultimately they are no longer even "produced" (by Nature), but immediately "reproduced": reproduction is the very being of Modernity.

We come full circle: not only is Pop Art an art, not only is this art ontological, but even its reference is finally—as in the highest periods of classical art—Nature; not of course the vegetal, scenic, or human (psychological) Nature: Nature today is the social absolute, or better still (for we are not directly concerned with politics) the Gregarious. This new Nature is accommodated by Pop Art, and moreover, whether it likes it or not, or rather whether it admits it or not, Pop Art criticizes this Nature. How? By imposing a *distance* upon its gaze (and hence upon our own). Even if all Pop artists have not had a privileged relation with Brecht (as was Warhol's case during the sixties), all of them practice, with regard to the object, that repository of the social relation, a kind of "distancing" which has a critical value. However, less naïve or less optimistic than Brecht, Pop Art neither formulates nor resolves its criticisms: to pose the object "flat out" is to pose the object at a distance, but it is also to refuse to say how this distance might be corrected. A cold confusion is imparted to the consistency of the gregarious world (a "mass" world); the disturbance of our gaze is as "matte" as the thing represented—and perhaps all the more terrible for that. In all the (re-)productions of Pop Art, one question threatens, challenges: *"What do you mean?"* (title of a poster by Allen Jones). This is the millennial question of that very old thing: Art.

POP—AN ART OF CONSUMPTION?
JEAN BAUDRILLARD

As we have seen,[1] the logic of consumption can be defined
as a manipulation of signs. The symbolic relation of interiority,
the symbolic relations of creation are absent from it: it is all
exteriority. The object loses its objective finality, its function,
and becomes the term of a much wider combinatory, of groups
of objects where its value is one of relation. Furthermore, it
loses its symbolic meaning, its age-old anthropomorphic status, and tends to dissipate in a discourse of connotations, which
are themselves also relative to one another within the framework of a totalitarian cultural system, that is to say, one which
is able to integrate significations from anywhere.

We have taken as our basis the analysis of *everyday*
objects. But there is another discourse on the object, that of art.
A history of the evolution of the status of objects and their
representation in art and literature would be revealing on its
own. After having traditionally played a wholly symbolic and
decorative role in art, objects in the 20th century have ceased to
be tied to moral or psychological values, they have ceased to
live by proxy in the shadow of man and have begun to assume
an extraordinary importance as autonomous elements in an

analysis of space (cubism, etc.) Thus they have dispersed, to the very point of abstraction. Having feted their parodic resurrection in Dada and Surrealism, destructured and volatilized by the Abstract, now they are apparently reconciled with their image in Nouvelle Figuration and Pop Art. It is here that the question of their contemporary status is raised: it is further brought to our attention by this sudden rise of objects to the zenith of artistic figuration.

In a word: is Pop Art the contemporary art form of that logic of signs and of their consumption which is being discussed here, or is it only an effect of fashion and thus purely an object of consumption itself? The two are not contradictory. One can grant that Pop Art transposes an object-world while quite accepting that it also results (according to its own logic) in objects pure and simple. Advertising shares the same ambiguity.

Let us formulate the question another way: the logic of consumption eliminates the traditional sublime status of artistic representation. Quite literally, there is no longer any privileging of the object over the image in essence or signification. One is no longer the truth of the other: they coexist *in extenso* and in the very same logical space, where they equally "act" as signs[2] (in their differential, reversible, combinatory relation). Whereas all art up to Pop was based on a vision of the world "in depth,"[3] Pop itself claims to be homogeneous with that *immanent order of signs*—homogeneous with their industrial and serial production, and thus with the artificial, manufactured character of the whole environment—homogeneous with the *in extenso* saturation as much as culturalized abstraction of this new order of things.

Does it succeed in "rendering" this systematic secularization of objects, in "rendering" this new descriptive environment in all its exteriority—such that nothing remains of the "inner light" which gave prestige to all earlier art? Is it an *art of the non-sacred*, that is to say, an art of pure manipulation? Is it itself a non-sacred art, that is to say productive and not creative of objects?

Some will say (and Pop artists themselves) that things are rather more simple. They do the thing because they are taken with it; after all, they're having a good time, they look around and paint what they see—it's spontaneous realism, etc. This is false: Pop signifies the end of perspective, the end of evocation, the end of witnessing, the end of the creative gesture and, not least of all, the end of the subversion of the world and of the malediction of art. Not only is its aim the immanence of the "civilized" world, but its total integration in this world. Here there is an insane ambition: that of abolishing the annals (and the foundations) of a whole culture, that of transcendence. Perhaps there is also quite simply an ideology. Let us clear away two objections: "It is an American art"—in its object material (including the obsession with "stars and stripes") in its empirical pragmatic, optimistic practice, in the incontestably chauvinist infatuation of certain patrons and collectors who are "taken in" by it, etc. Even though this objection is tendentious, let us reply objectively: if all this is *Americanism,* Pop artists can only adopt it according to their own logic. If manufactured objects "speak American," it is because they have no other truth than this mythology which overwhelms them—and the only logical course is to integrate this mythological discourse and to be integrated in it oneself. If the consumer society is caught up in its own mythology, if it has no critical perspective on itself, and *if this is precisely its definition,*[4] then no contemporary art can exist which, in its very existence and practice, is not compromised by, party to this opaque obviousness of things. Indeed, this is why Pop artists paint objects according to their real appearance, since it is *only thus, as readymade signs, "fresh from the assembly line," that they function mythologically.* This is why they preferably paint the initials, marks, slogans borne by these objects and why, ultimately, they can paint only that (Robert Indiana). Not as a game or as "realism," but a recognition of the obvious fact of consumer society: namely, that the truth of objects and products is their *mark.* If that is "Americanism," then Americanism is the very logic of contemporary culture, and Pop artists could hardly be reproached for making it evident.

No more than they could be reproached for their commercial success, and for accepting it without shame. Even worse, condemned and thus reinvested with a sacred function. It is logical for an art that does not oppose the world of objects but explores its system, to enter itself into the system. It is even the end of a certain hypocrisy and radical illogicality. In contrast with earlier painting (since the end of the 19th century), *signed* and commercialized in terms of the signature (the Abstract Expressionists carried this triumphant inspiration and this shameless opportunism to a higher plane), Pop artists reconcile the object of painting and the painting-object. Coherence or paradox? Through its predilection for objects, through this infinite figuration of "marked" objects and material consumables, and through its commercial success, Pop Art

36

is the first to explore the status of its own art-object as "signed" and "consumed."

Yet this logical enterprise, whose extreme consequences one would not but applaud were they to contravene our traditional *moral* aesthetic, is coupled with an ideology into which it is not far from sinking. An ideology of Nature, of an Awakening ("Wake Up") and of authenticity, which evokes the best moments of bourgeois spontaneity.

This "radical empiricism," "uncompromising positivism," "antiteleologism" (Mario Amaya, *Pop as Art*) sometimes assumes a dangerously *initiatic* aspect. Oldenburg: "I drove around the city one day with Jimmy Dine. By chance we drove through Orchard Street, both sides of which are packed with small stores. As we drove I remember having a vision of 'The Store.' I saw, in my mind's eye, a complete environment based on this theme. Again it seemed to me that I had discovered a new world, I began wandering through stores—all kinds and all over—*as though they were museums*. I saw objects displayed in windows and on counters as precious works of art." Rosenquist: "Then suddenly, the ideas seemed to flow towards me through the window. All I had to do was seize them on the wing and start painting. Everything spontaneously fell into place—the idea, the composition, the images, the colors, everything started to work on its own." It appears that, on the theme of "Inspiration," Pop artists are in no way inferior to earlier generations. This theme implies, since Werther, the ideality of a *Nature* to which it suffices to be faithful in order that it be true. It is simply necessary to awaken it, reveal it. We read in John Cage, musician and theorist-inspirator of Rauschenberg and Jasper Johns: " . . . art should be an affirmation—

not an attempt to bring order . . . but simply a way of *waking up* to the very life we are living, which is so excellent, once one gets one's mind and one's desires out of the way and lets it act of its own accord." This acquiescence to a revealed order—the universe of images and of manufactured objects shining through to a basic *nature*—leads to professions of a mystico-realist faith: "A flag was just a flag, a number was simply a number" (Jasper Johns), or again John Cage: "We must set about discovering a means to let sounds be themselves"— which assumes an essence of the object, a level of absolute reality which is never that of the everyday environment, and which with regard to it constitutes quite frankly a surreality. Wesselmann thus speaks of the "superreality" of an ordinary kitchen.

In brief, we are in total confusion, and we find ourselves before a kind of behaviorism arising from a juxtaposition of visible things (something like an impressionism of consumer society) coupled with a vague Zen or Buddhist mystique of stripping down the Ego and Super-ego to the "Id" of the surrounding world. There is also Americanism in this curious mixture!

But above all there is a grave equivocation and inconsistency. For by not presenting the surrounding world for what it is, that is to say, primarily an artificial field of manipulable signs, a total cultural artifact where what comes into play is not sensation or vision, but a differential perception and a tactical game of significations—by presenting it as revealed nature, as essence, Pop has a double connotation: first, as the ideology of an integrated society (contemporary society=nature=ideal society—but we've seen that this collusion is part of its logic);

and on the other hand, it reinstates the whole *sacred process of art*, which destroys its basic objective.

Pop wants to be the art of the commonplace (this is the very reason it calls itself Popular Art): but what is the commonplace if not a metaphysical category, a modern version of the category of the sublime? The object is only commonplace in its use, at the moment when it is used (Wesselmann's transistor "that walks"). The object ceases to be commonplace the moment it signifies: as we have seen, the "truth" of the contemporary object is no longer to be useful for something, but to signify; no longer to be manipulated as an instrument, but as a sign. And the success of Pop, in the best instances, is that it shows it to us as such.

Andy Warhol, whose approach is the most radical, is also the one who best epitomizes the theoretical contradictions in the practice of this painting, and the difficulties the latter has in envisaging its true object. He says: "The canvas is an entirely ordinary object, as much as this chair or this poster" (always that will to absorb, to reabsorb art, revealing both American pragmatism—terrorism of the useful, blackmail of integration—and something like an echo of the mystique of sacrifice). He adds: "Reality needs no intermediary, one simply has to isolate it from its surroundings and put it down on the canvas." Now that is the whole question in point: for the ordinariness of this chair (or hamburger, car fin or pin-up face) is exactly its context, and mainly the serial context of all similar or slightly dissimilar chairs, etc. Ordinariness is *the difference in repetition.* By isolating the chair on the canvas, I relieve it of all ordinariness, and, at the same time, I relieve the canvas of its whole character as an everyday object (by which, according to Warhol, it should have absolutely resembled the chair). Such an impasse is well known: art can no more be absorbed in the everyday (canvas=chair) than it can grasp the everyday as such (the chair isolated on the canvas=the real chair). Immanence and transcendence are equally impossible: they are two sides of the same dream.

In short, there is no essence of the everyday, of the ordinary, and thus no art of the everyday: this is a mystical aporia. If Warhol (and others) believe in it, this is because they delude themselves with regard to the very status of art and of the artistic act—which is not at all rare among artists. Moreover, with regard to the mystical nostalgia at the very level of the act, of the productive gesture: "I want to be a machine," says Warhol, who paints in effect by stenciling, screen-printing, etc. Now, for art to pose as machine-like is the worst kind of vanity, and for whoever enjoys—willingly or not—the status of creator to dedicate himself to serial automatism is the greatest affectation. Yet it is difficult to accuse either Warhol or the Pop artists of bad faith: their exacting logic collides with a certain sociological and cultural status of art, about which they can do nothing. It is this powerlessness which their ideology conveys. When they try to desacralize their practice, society sacralizes them all the more. Added to which is the fact that their attempt—however radical it might be—to secularize art, in its themes and its practice, leads to an exaltation and an unprecedented manifestation of the sacred in art. Quite simply, Pop artists forget that for the picture not to become a sacred super-sign (a unique object, a signature, an object of noble and magical commerce), the author's content or intentions are not enough: it is the structures of culture production which are decisive. In the end, only rationalizing, like any manufacturer, the market for painting could desacralize it and return the picture to everyday objects.[5] Perhaps this is neither thinkable nor possible nor even desirable—who knows? In any event, it is a borderline situation: once there, either you stop painting or you continue at the cost of regressing into the traditional mythology of artistic creation. And through this sliding, the classical pictorial values are retrieved: Oldenburg's "expressionist" treatment, Wesselmann's fauvist and Matissian one, Lichtenstein's "art nouveau" and Japanese calligraphy, etc. What have we to do with these legendary resonances? What have we to do with these effects which say, "It's still all the same painting?" The logic of Pop is elsewhere, not in an aesthetic computation or a metaphysics of the object.

Pop could be defined as a *game,* and a manipulation, of different levels of mental perception: a kind of mental cubism which seeks to diffract objects not according to a spatial analysis, but according to modalities of perception elaborated throughout the centuries on the basis of a whole culture's intellectual and technological apparatus: objective reality, image-reflection, figuration by drawing, technological figuration (the photo), abstract schematization, the discursive utterance, etc. On the other hand, the use of the phonetic alphabet and industrial techniques have imposed schemes of division, doubling, abstraction, repetition (ethnographers tell of the Primitives' bewilderment upon discovering several books *absolutely* alike: their whole vision of the world is turned upside down). In these various modes one can see the myriad figures of a *rhetoric of designation*, of recognition. And this is where Pop comes into play: it works on the differences

41

between these different levels or modes, and on the perception of these differences. Thus the screenprint of a lynching is not an evocation: it presupposes this lynching transmuted into a news item, into a journalistic sign by virtue of mass communications—a sign taken to yet another level by screen-printing. The same photo repeated presupposes the unique photo, and, beyond that, the real being whose reflection it is: moreover, this real being could figure in the work without destroying it—it would only be one more combination.

Just as there is no order of reality in Pop Art, but levels of signification, there is no real space—the only space is that of the canvas, that of the juxtaposition of different elements/signs and of their relations; neither is there any real time—the only time is that of the reading, that of the differential perception of the object and its image, of such an image and the same repeated, etc., the time necessary for a *mental correction*, for an *accommodation* to the image, to the artifact in its relation to the real object (it is not a question of a reminiscence, but of the perception of a *local, logical* difference). Neither is this reading searching for an articulation or a coherence, but a coverage *in extenso*, a statement of successive order.

It can be seen that the activity Pop prescribes (once again, in its ambition of rigor) is far from our "aesthetic sensibility." Pop is a "cool" art: it requires neither aesthetic ecstasy nor affective or symbolic participation ("deep involvement"), but a kind of abstract involvement or *instrumental curiosity*. Retaining a little of that child-like curiosity or naïve enchantment of discovery—and why not?—Pop can also be seen as comic-book religious images, or as a Book of Hours of consumption, but which above all brings into play intellectual reflexes of decoding, of deciphering, etc., those of which we will come to speak.

In conclusion, Pop Art is not a popular art. For the popular culture ethos (if that indeed exists) rests precisely on an unambiguous realism, on linear narration (and not on repetition or the diffraction of levels), on allegory and the decorative (this is not Pop Art, since these two categories refer back to "something" essential), and on emotive participation linked to the moral of life's uncertainties.[6] It is only on a rudimentary level that Pop Art can be understood as a "figurative" art: a colored imagery, a naïve chronicle of consumer society, etc. It is true that Pop artists are also happy to claim this. Their candor is immense, as is their ambiguity. With regard to their humor, or to that attributed to them, here again we are on unstable ground. It would be instructive, in this regard, to register the reactions of viewers. With many, the works provoke a laughter (or at least the inclination to a laughter) which is moral and obscene (these canvases are obscene in the classical view). Then, a smile of derision, but whether it judges the objects painted or the painting itself it is difficult to know. A smile which becomes a willing accomplice: "That can't be serious, but we are not going to be scandalized, and after all perhaps..." All more or less twisted up in the shameful desolation of not knowing how to take it. That said, Pop is at once full of humor and humorless. In all logic it has nothing to do with subversive, aggressive humor, with the telescoping of surrealist objects. It is not at all concerned to short-circuit objects in their function, but to juxtapose them in order to analyze their relations. This move is not terrorist;[7] rather, at the very most, it conveys effects derived from cultural isolation. In fact, it is a question of

43

something else. Let us not forget, by taking us back to the system described, that a *"certain smile"* is one of the *obligatory signs* of consumption: it no longer indicates a humor, a critical distance, but only recalls that transcendent critical value materialized today in a knowing wink. This false distance is everywhere, in spy films, with Godard, in modern advertising which continually uses it as a cultural allusion, etc. Ultimately, in this "cool" smile, you can no longer distinguish between the smile of humor and that of commercial complicity. This is what also happens in Pop Art—after all, its smile epitomizes its whole ambiguity: it is not the smile of critical distance, it is the smile of *collusion*.

Notes:

1) This text is taken from Jean Baudrillard, *La société de consommation: ses mythes, ses structures*, Paris, Gallimard, 1970, pp. 174-185—from the section entitled "La culture mass-médiatique."

2) Cf. Boorstin, *The Image*.

3) The Cubists: again, it is the "essence" of space which they seek, an unveiling of the "secret geometry," etc. Dada or Duchamp or the Surrealists: here objects are stripped of their (bourgeois) function and made to stand out in their subversive banality, recalling the lost essence and an order of authenticity evoked by the absurd. Ponge: his seizing upon the naked and concrete object is still a poetic consciousness or perception in action. In brief, all art "without which things would only be what they are" feeds (before Pop) on transcendence.

4) Cf. below: *The Consumption of Consumption*.

5) In this sense, the truth of Pop concerns the earning capacity and promotion, not the contract and the gallery of painting.

6) "Popular" art is not attached to objects, but always primarily to man and his exploits. It would not paint a delicatessen or the American flag, but a-man-eating or a-man-saluting-the-American-flag.

7) In fact, we often read this "terrorist" humor into it. But through a critical nostalgia on our part.

THE CULTURAL POLITICS OF POP
ANDREAS HUYSSEN

In the mid 1960s, when the student movement broadened its criticism of the university system to include attacks on West German society, politics and institutions in general, a wave of Pop enthusiasm swept the Federal Republic. The notion of Pop that attracted people almost magically not only referred to the new art by Warhol, Lichtenstein, Wesselmann and others; it also stood for beat and rock music, poster art, the flower child cult and drug scene—indeed for any manifestation of "subculture" and "underground." In short, Pop became the synonym for the new life style of the younger generation, a life style which rebelled against authority and sought liberation from the norms of existing society. As an "emancipation euphoria" spread, mainly among high school and university students, Pop in its broadest sense became amalgamated with the public and political activities of the anti-authoritarian New Left.

Consequently, the conservative press once more decried the general decay of Western culture, not deeming it necessary to investigate whether the protest—political or apolitical— was in any way legitimate. The traditionally conservative cultural critics reacted accordingly. Since they preferred to meditate in seclusion about Kafka and Kandinsky, experimental literature and abstract expressionism, they denounced Pop Art as non-art, supermarket-art, Kitsch-art and as a coca-colonization of Western Europe.[1] But various branches of industry and business (producing and marketing records, posters, films, textiles) understood immediately that the youth movement created needs that could be exploited economically. New markets opened up for cheap silkscreens and small sized graphic works. Mini-galleries were inaugurated as frequently as mini-boutiques.[2] The art experts, of course, continued to feud about whether Pop Art should or should not be accepted as a legitimate form of art.

Meanwhile, a predominantly young art audience had begun to interpret American Pop Art as protest and criticism rather than the affirmation of an affluent society.[3] It would be worthwhile to examine why this view of Pop as critical art was much more widespread in Germany than in the United States. The strong German tradition of culture criticism (*Kulturkritik*) certainly has something to do with the difference in reception; another factor, however, was that in Germany the Pop reception coincided with the student movement, while in the United States Pop preceded university unrest. When Pop artists exhibited commodities or declared that serial productions of Coca-Cola bottles, film stars or comic strips were art works, many Germans did not see these works as affirmative reproductions of mass produced reality; they preferred to think that this art was intended to denounce the lack of values and criteria in art criticism and that it sought to close the gap between high or serious, and low or light, art. The works themselves only partially suggested such an interpretation, but it was strengthened by the needs and interests of individual recipients, determined as they were by age, class, origin, and contraditions of consciousness. The interpretation of Pop as critical art was certainly fostered in Europe by the fact that European artists of the 1960s, whose works were often exhibited together with American Pop works, were indeed trying to develop an art of social criticism. The crucial factor, however, was the atmosphere created by anti-authoritarian protest and its adherence to Marcuse's cultural theories, an atmosphere that cast an aura of social criticism over many cultural phenomena which appear quite different from today's perspective.

When I saw the Pop *Documenta* in Kassel in 1968 and the famous Ludwig collection on exhibit in Cologne's Wallraf-Richartz-Museum, I found sensuous appeal and excitement not only in the works by Rauschenberg and Johns, but especially in those by Warhol, Lichtenstein, Wesselmann, and Indiana. I, like many others, believed that Pop Art could be the beginning of a far-reaching democratization of art and art appreciation. This reaction was as spontaneous as it was false. Right or wrong notwithstanding, the very real feeling of liberation which many art spectators experienced at that time was more important: Pop seemed to liberate art from the monumental boredom of Informel and Abstract Expressionism; it seemed to break through the confines of the ivory tower in which art had been going around in circles in the 1950s. It seemed to ridicule the deadly serious art criticism which never acknowledged fantasy, play, and spontaneity. Pop's almost indiscriminate use of bright colors was overwhelming. I was won over by its obvious enjoyment of play, its focus on our daily environment, and at the same time by what I took to be its implied critique of this same environment. Art audiences were expanding considerably. In the 1950s, most art exhibits had been exclusive events for a small circle of experts and buyers. In the 1960s, hundreds, even thousands of people came to the opening of a single exhibition. No longer did exhibitions take place only in small galleries; modern art invaded the big art institutes and museums. Of course, it was still a bourgeois audience, including many young people, many students. But one was tempted to believe that the expansion of interest in art would be unlimited. As for the derogatory and condemning judgments by conservative critics, they only seemed to prove that the new art was indeed radical and progressive. The belief in consciousness-raising by means of aesthetic experience was quite common in those days.

Still something else recommended this art to the younger generation. The "realism" of Pop Art, it closeness to objects, images and reproductions of everyday life, stimulated a new debate about the relationship between art and life, image and reality, a debate that filled the culture pages of the national newspapers and weeklies. Pop seemed to liberate high art from the isolation in which it had been kept in the bourgeois society. Art's distance "from the rest of the world and the rest of experience"[4] was to be eliminated. A new avenue seemed to lead almost by necessity to the bridging of the traditional gap between high and low art. From the very beginning, Pop proclaimed that it would eliminate the historical separation between the aesthetic and the nonaesthetic, thereby joining and reconciling art and reality. The secularization of art seemed to have reached a new stage at which the work of art rid itself of the remnants of its origins in magic and rite. In bourgeois ideology, the work of art—in spite of its almost complete detachment from ritual—still functioned as a kind of substitute for religion; with Pop, however, art became profane, concrete and suitable for mass reception. Pop Art seemed to have the potential to become a genuinely "popular" art and to resolve the crisis of bourgeois art, which had been evident since the beginning of this century.

The Crisis of Bourgeois Art: Adorno and Marcuse

Those who had confidence in the critical nature and emancipatory effect of Pop Art were well aware of this crisis of bourgeois art. In Thomas Mann's *Doctor Faustus* it results in the pact between the composer Adrian Leverkühn and the devil, whose help became a prerequisite for all of Leverkühn's compositions. In the novel the devil speaks as an art critic: "But the sickness is general, and the straightforward ones shew the symptoms just as well as the producers of backformations. Does not production threaten to come to an end? And whatever of serious stuff gets on to paper betrays effort and distaste . . . Composing itself has got too hard, devilishly hard. Where work does not go any longer with sincerity how is one to work? But so it stands, my friend, the masterpiece, the self-sufficient form, belongs to traditional art, emancipated art rejects it."[5] Why, one asks, has composing become so difficult? Why is the masterwork a thing of the past? Changes in society? The devil answers: "True, but unimportant. The prohibitive difficulties of the work lie deep in the work itself.

The historical movement of the musical material has turned against the self-contained work."[6] The emancipated art on which Thomas Mann's devil elaborates is still a highly complex art which can neither break out of its isolation nor resolve the radical opposition of aesthetic illusion (*Schein*) and reality. It is well known that Thomas Mann took ideas from Adorno's philosophy of music and integrated them into the novel. The devil speaks Adorno's mind. Adorno himself always insisted on the separation of art and reality. For him, serious art could only negate the negativity of reality. It is only through negation, he believed, that the work mantains its independence, its autonomy, its claim to truth. Adorno found such negation in the intricate writings of Kafka and Beckett, in the prohibitively difficult music of Schönberg and Berg. After reading Thomas Mann's novel one might come to the conclusion that the crisis of the art takes place in a realm hermetically sealed off from the outer world and from the production relations of art that any modern artist must deal with. But Adorno's arguments have to be understood within the framework of his analysis of culture industry, which is contained in his *Dialektik der Aufklärung* (1947), co-authored with Max Horkheimer.[7] To Adorno, it seemed necessary and unavoidable that serious art negate reality; this view was a result of his American experiences, which convinced him that in the modern, rationally organized capitalistic state even culture loses its independence and is deprived of its critical substance. The manipulative praxis of this culture industry—Adorno thought mainly of record, film, and radio production—subordinates all spiritual and intellectual creation to the profit motive. Adorno again summed up his conclusions—equally pessimistic for high and low art—in a 1963 radio lecture: "Culture industry is the purposeful integration of its consumers from above. It also forces a reconciliation of high and low art, which have been separated for thousands of years, a reconciliation which damages both. High art is deprived of its seriousness because its effect is programmed; low art is put in chains and deprived of the unruly resistance inherent in it when social control was not yet total."[8] It follows that art in a traditional sense has become inconceivable today.

Certainly the Pop enthusiasts of the 1960s found less support in Adorno's thesis of total manipulation than in Marcuse's demand for a sublation (*Aufhebung*) of culture which they believed Pop Art was about to initiate. In his essay "The Affirmative Character of Culture," which was first printed in 1937 in the *Zeitschrift für Sozialforschung* and republished by Suhrkamp in 1965, Marcuse reproached classical bourgeois art for secluding itself from the realities of social labor and economic competition and for creating a world of beautiful illusion, the supposedly autonomous realm of aesthetics which fulfills longings for a happy life and satisfies human needs only in an unreal and illusory way: "There is a good reason for the exemplification of the cultural ideal in art, for only in art has bourgeois society tolerated its own ideals and taken them seriously as a general demand. What counts as utopia, fantasy and rebellion in the world of fact is allowed in art. There affirmative culture has displayed the forgotten truths over which 'realism' triumphs in daily life. The medium of beauty decontaminates truth and sets it apart from the present. What occurs in art occurs with no obligation."[9] Marcuse believed that the utopia of a better life expressed in bourgeois art need only be taken at its word. Then, by necessity, the autonomy of art would be eliminated and art would be integrated into the material life process. This elimination of affirmative culture would go together with a revolution of the patterns of bourgeois life: "Beauty will find a new embodiment when it no longer is represented as real illusion but, instead, expresses reality and joy in reality."[10] Habermas has pointed out that in 1937, in view of fascist mass art, Marcuse could have had no delusions about the possibility of a false sublation of culture.[11] But thirty years later, the student revolt in the United States, France and Germany seemed to be initiating precisely the transformation of culture and the radical change of life patterns which Marcuse had once hoped for.[12]

Since Pop Art had a strong impact in the Federal Republic only in the second half of the 1960s, its reception coincided with the high point of the anti-authoritarian revolt and with attempts to create a new culture. This would explain why Pop Art was accepted in the Federal Republic (but not in the United States) as an ally in the struggle against traditional bourgeois culture, and why many people believed that Pop Art fulfilled Marcuse's demand that art not be illusion but express reality and the joy in reality. There is an unresolved contradiction inherent in this interpretation of Pop Art: how was it possible that an art expressing sensuous joy in our daily environment could at the same time be critical of this environment? One might also ask to what extent Marcuse was misunderstood on these matters. It remains highly doubtful whether Marcuse would have interpreted Pop Art as a sublation of culture. It is true that Marcuse spoke of the integration of culture into the material life process, but he never explained this idea in detail. If this deficiency is one side of the coin, the other is Marcuse's insistence on bourgeois idealistic aesthetics. An example: when Marcuse praises the songs of Bob Dylan, he lifts them out of the material life process and sees in them the promise for a liberated, utopian society of the future. Marcuse's emphasis on this anticipatory, utopian role of the work of art owes as much to bourgeois aesthetics as does Adorno's thesis of the work of art as a total negation of existing reality. But it was just this idealism in Marcuse's thought that appealed to the early student movement, and his influence on the Pop reception in the Federal Republic makes Pop's links with the anti-authoritarian revolt evident.

Warhol and Duchamp: A Disgression into Art History

Some observations on art history might be appropriate before moving on to the second phase of Pop reception in the Federal Republic—the critical evaluation of Pop by the New Left, which will have to be discussed in the context of the larger art debate after 1968.

In 1962 Andy Warhol, who is seen as the most representative Pop artist in the Federal Republic,[13] "painted" a series of serial portraits of Marilyn Monroe. I pick one of them for discussion: five times five frontal views of the actress' face arranged in rectangular order. Warhol has chosen one photo and reproduced it with the silk screen technique,[14] adding slight modifications to the original. Art thus becomes the reproduction of a reproduction. It is not reality itself that provides the content of the work of art, but rather a secondary reality—the portrait of the mass idol as the cliché image that appears millions of times in the mass media and that sinks into the consciousness of a mass audience. The work is made up of identical elements and characterized by a simple, theoretically unlimited, serial structure. The artist has surrendered to the principles of anonymous mass reproduction and has documented his closeness to the image world of the mass media. Affirmation or critique—that is the question. By itself, the artistic structure of the Monroe silk screen hardly provides an answer.

One year later, in 1963, Warhol created a similiar serial portrait with the revealing title *Thirty are better than one*. This time the subject was not an idol of mass culture, but a reproduction of Leonardo da Vinci's *Mona Lisa*, not even in color, but in the black and white of photography. The Renaissance artist's masterpiece has its renaissance under the production conditions of modern media society. But Warhol not only cites Leonardo's work which, due to its mass distribution in the form of prints, could be considered part of today's mass culture.[15] He also alludes to one of the fathers of the art of the 1960s—Marcel Duchamp, himself an elite artist par excellence.

In 1919 Duchamp took a reproduction of Leonardo's *Mona Lisa*, pencilled in a moustache and a goatee, and called this "combination ready-made"[16] *L.H.O.O.Q.*, initials which reveal the iconoclastic intention of the work if pronounced in French (elle a chaud au cul, or she has a hot ass).[17] Of course, the "creator" of the ready-mades mainly wanted to provoke and shock a society which had gone bankrupt in World War I.

It is not the artistic achievement of Leonardo that is ridiculed by moustache, goatee and obscene allusion, but rather the cult object the *Mona Lisa* had become in that temple of bourgeois art religion, the Louvre. Duchamp challenged the traditional concepts of beauty, creativity, originality, and autonomy still more boldly in 1917, when he declared as a work of art an object designed for reproduction—a urinal, which he called *Fountain* and signed with a pseudonym. An *objet trouvé*, the urinal becomes a work of art only by virtue of the fact that an artist exhibits it. In those days, the audience recognized the provocation and was shocked. It understood all too well that Dada attacked all the holy cows of bourgeois art-religion. And yet Dada's frontal attack was unsuccessful, not only because the movement exhausted itself in negation, but also because even then bourgeois culture was able to co-opt any kind of attack made on it. Duchamp himself saw this dilemma and withdrew from the art scene in 1923. The withdrawal seems only logical considering that today an assiduous audience admires *L.H.O.O.Q.* as a masterpiece of modernism in the museum.

When there was a New York retrospective of his work in 1965, Duchamp once again tried to express the problem artistically. As invitations to the opening, he sent out one hundred post-Warholian Mona Lisas. They depicted a Mona Lisa without moustache and goatee on the backside of a playing card bearing the title *Rasé L.H.O.O.Q.* "Through this reconstruction of her identity the Mona Lisa has as a matter of fact completely lost her identity,"[18] the critic Max Imdahl commented. I rather ask myself whether the "certain smile" of the *Mona Lisa* is not ironically directed at an audience that accepts the mere repetition of a provocation as art[19] or that can revel in the thought that today even provocation has become a cliché. Did Duchamp, who never concealed his disapproval of Pop, not see that the outrage of 1919 had degenerated into applause and co-option? Warhol, to be sure, is more consistent in this matter. He does not even want to provoke anymore. He simply reproduces mass reproduced reality like Coca-Cola bottles, Brillo boxes, photos of filmstars, and Campbell Soup cans. In his polemic against the distinction between non-art and art the dadaist Duchamp still sides with art *ex negativo* (almost all of his post-Dada work bears witness to this), but Warhol is no longer even interested in such a polemic.[20] This becomes clear in interviews in which his statements are closer to the language of commercial advertising than to any form of art criticism. The following passage, taken from an interview conducted by G.R. Swenson in 1963, shows how Warhol naïvely praises the reification of modern life as a virtue: "Someone said that Brecht wanted everybody to think alike. I want everybody to think alike. But Brecht wanted to do it through Communism, in a way. Russia is doing it under government: it's happening here all by itself without being under a strict government; so if it's working without trying, why can't it work without being communist? Everybody looks alike and acts alike, and we're getting more and more that way. I think everybody should be a machine. I think everybody should like everybody. *Is that what Pop Art is all about?* Yes. It's liking things."[21] Warhol seems to be a victim of the advertising slogans he himself helped design before he became an artist. He had made the switch from ad man to artist with a single idea: not to advertise products, but to proclaim those same products and their graphic reproductions as works of art. In accordance with Warhol's slogan "All is pretty," the Pop artists took the trivial and banal imagery of daily life at face value, and the subjugation of art by the laws of a commodity-producing capitalistic society seemed complete.

Criticism of Pop Art

It is exactly at this point that criticism set in. Pop artists were accused of surrendering to the capitalist mode of production in their techniques and of glorifying the commodity marked by their choice of subject.[22] Frequently such criticism took issue with Warhol's soup cans, Lichtenstein's comics, Wesselmann's bathroom arrangements. It was pointed out that several Pop artists had worked in advertising and graphic design before coming to art and that the difference between advertisement and art shrunk to a minimum in many of their works—a fact which is not to be mistaken for the elimination of the art-life dichotomy. Furthermore, it was observed that Pop Art, which partly originated in advertising, in turn influenced it. Comics, for instance, began appearing in ads only after Lichtenstein had made them the main theme of his work.[23] The mouth canvases of Wesselmann, themselves part of the lipstick and toothpaste ad tradition, had a visible effect on such ads. While ads of an earlier period showed the human being belonging to those lips and teeth, post-Wesselmann ads frequently blow up the mouth and show nothing but the mouth.[24] It is symptomatic that the artists themselves did not see this link between Pop and advertising as something negative. James Rosenquist, for instance, who also came to art from advertising, stated: "I think we have a free society, and the action that goes on in this free society allows encroachments, as a commercial society. So I geared myself, like an advertiser or a large company, to this visual inflation—in commercial advertising which is one of the foundations of our society. I'm living in it, and it has such impact and excitement in its means of imagery."[25] Of course it is problematic to take such self-interpretation by artists too literally. There are quite a few cases in the history of art and literature where a work revealed an intention or a tendency which blatantly contradicted the artist's ideological consciousness. But subtle doubts did not seem appropriate at a time when the theoretical discussion of art had led to a radical skepticism toward all contemporary art, including Pop. Pop Art in particular had contributed to this radical skepticism—not as the new art of an imaginary cultural revolution which some of Pop's disciples hoped for, but rather as an art that revealed the elitist and esoteric nature of traditional avant-gardism because more than any other preceding art movement it laid bare the commodity character of all contemporary art production.[26]

Art as Commodity

It is not surprising that the left's criticism focused on the commodity character of art in capitalistic society. Forums for discussion were *Kursbuch* 15 with essays by Karl Markus Michel, Hans Magnus Enzensberger and Walter Bölich, and

Die Zeit, which printed an analysis by the Berlin SDS collective "Culture and Revolution," programmatically entitled "Art as Commodity of the Consciousness Industry."[27] This theoretical discussion, in which different positions of the New Left were articulated independently from each other, bears on the critical evaluation of Pop Art even though Pop was mentioned neither in the SDS paper nor in *Kursbuch*.

The SDS collective's point of departure is the thesis that every individually produced and supposedly autonomous work of art is swallowed up by the system of distribution (art dealers, galleries, museums). Not only does the artist depend on efficient organization of the distribution apparatus, but even the reception of the work of art takes place within the framework of the culture industry. By advertising and promoting the works it distributes, the industry generates certain expectations. The aesthetic objectivation achieved in the work of art does not reach the consumer directly; it is filtered through the mode of mediation. The culture industry—which like any other branch of industry is integrated into the economic system of capitalist society—is thus the pivot of art production and art reception. In apparent agreement with Adorno, the SDS collective concludes: "Art, caught up in the distribution system of culture industry, is subjected to the ideology of supply and demand. It becomes commodity. The culture industry sees the legitimation of producing art only in art's exchange value, not in its use value. In other words, the objective content of art works and their enlightening role become irrelevant in a system based on profit maximization, against which an adequate reception of art would rebel."[28] While low art (Hollywood movies, TV series, bestsellers, hit parades) floods the consumer with positive models which are as abstract as they are unrealistic, the function of high art is to legitimize bourgeois domination in the cultural realm by intimidating the non-specialist, i.e., the majority of a given population. With this evaluation of high art, the SDS analysis goes beyond Adorno, who also condemns the culture industry, but keeps insisting that if high art rejects economic utilization, it can offer the only realm of withdrawal for creative, non-alienated labor. In the SDS analysis, the culture industry's capability for manipulation seems complete. The analysis in effect combines Adorno's attack on low, trivial art with a version of Marcuse's thesis of the affirmative character of high art—a reductionist version, in which high art, viewed as nothing but a means of domination, is deprived of its utopian and anticipatory element.

Given such a gloomy description of the situation, the conclusions reached by the SDS theoreticians seem contradictory. Suddenly they demand that bourgeois aesthetics be dealt with critically—as if the culture industry had not already made bourgeois aesthetics obsolete. They also call for the creation of a progressive art, though clearly it could only be a critique of a negative reality—again a critique of ideology *(Ideologiekritik)*. These suggestions are clearly products of a period in the student movement when it was believed that enlightenment would bring about a change of consciousness, that revolutionary change would take place in the superstructure. Which material forces would bring about this revolution was a question never answered. Despite the fact that at this time critical theory was already being vigorously criticized, the SDS paper documents a continued dependence on Adorno and Marcuse.

It focused not on the productive forces and the productive relations in the realm of art, but rather on problems of manipulation and consumption which the SDS collective hoped to solve by a critique of ideology.

Similiar difficulties emerge in the essays in *Kursbuch* 15 which are characterized by a capitulation to the consciousness industry and by the declaration that art and literature are dead. It is true that Enzensberger condemned the then fashionable *pompes funèbres* that celebrated the death of culture under the banner of a cultural revolution. But his analysis confirmed what at first he wanted to shrug off as a literary metaphor— the death of literature; more precisely, the death of *littérature engagée*, which saw social criticism as its main function, and which had dominated the German scene in the 1950s and early 1960s. This insight resulted largely from the student movement which, as Karl Markus Michel pointed out correctly in the same issue, had zeroed in on the social privileges of artists and writers, and had drawn attention to the distance separating artists from social praxis.[29] Enzensberger adopted this argument when he reproached engaged literature "for not uniting political demands and political praxis."[30] Maybe the left's enthusiasm for cultural revolution was somewhat naïve. Maybe Enzensberger was right in criticizing the revolutionary histrionics of the left which "by liquidating literature sought to compensate for its own incompetence."[31] But he should have seen that his desire "to teach Germany the alphabet of politics"[32] was not all that different from the intentions of the student left. After all, Enzensberger too demands a critical art and suggests documentary and reportage as appropriate literary genres. Like the SDS paper, Enzensberger's essay leaves open the question to what extent such a critical art could be effective in a culture whose main characteristic is manipulation."[33] A more basic question must be raised as to whether these critical essays do not run the risk of fetishizing the very notion of culture industry. How can one continually demand new forms of critical art if the culture industry in fact suppresses any enlightenment and criticism of capitalist society? How can Enzensberger get around the "law of the market" which "dominates literature perhaps even more than other products?"[34] Where art is seen as commodity and as nothing but commodity, there is an economic reductionism equating the relations of production with what is produced, the system of distribution with what is distributed, the reception of art with the consumption of all commodities. This is a misunderstanding. We cannot dogmatically reduce art to its exchange value, as if its use value were determined by the mode of distribution rather than by its content.[35] The theory of total manipulation underestimates the dialectical nature of art. Even under the conditions set by the capitalistic culture industry and its distribution apparatus, art ultimately can open up emancipatory avenues if only because it is granted autonomy and practical uselessness. The thesis of the total subjugation of art to the market also underestimates possibilities for emancipation inherent in consumption: in general, consumption satisfies needs, and even though human needs can be distorted to an amazing degree, every need contains a smaller or larger kernel of authenticity. The question to ask is how this kernel can be utilized and fulfilled.

The Benjamin Debate

Capitalist culture industry inevitably produces a minimum of art and a maximum of trash and kitsch. Therefore, the task is to change the culture industry itself. But how can it be done? Critical art alone does not suffice, since in the best of cases, its success remains limited to consciousness raising. As early as 1934, Walter Benjamin noted that "the bourgeois apparatus of production and publication is capable of assimilating, indeed of propagating, an astonishing amount of revolutionary themes without ever seriously putting into question its own continued existence or that of the class which owns it."[36] Critical Theory did not lead out of this dead end street. A return to Benjamin and Brecht, however, seemed to provide a new perspective and new possibilities. It is significant that in the Federal Republic interest in Benjamin initiated by Adorno's and Tiedemann's editions led to an attack on the Frankfurt editors. They were reproached with playing down the importance of Brecht and Marxism for the late Benjamin.[37]

Interest in Benjamin's theses about materialist aesthetics reached a high point after 1968, when the student movement left its anti-authoritarian phase and tried to develop socialist perspective going beyond "protest against the system" and the "great refusal." The notion of manipulation, on which Adorno's theory of culture industry and Marcuse's theory of one-dimensional man were based, was legitimately criticized, but the critique went too far, frequently ending up as a complete rejection of both Adorno and Marcuse. Their place was now taken by the Benjamin of the mid-1930s. Two of his essays, "The Author as Producer" and "The Work of Art in the Age of

63

Mechanical Reproduction," became particularly influential. It is worth mentioning that Adorno and Horkheimer had conceived the chapter on culture industry in *Dialektik der Aufklärung* as a reply to Benjamin's 1936 "reproduction" essay; the latter is also related to Marcuse's essay "The Affirmative Character of Culture," which, like Benjamin's piece, was first published in the *Zeitschrift für Sozialforschung*. Both essays deal with the sublation (*Aufhebung*) of bourgeois culture, albeit in very different ways.[38]

Benjamin was influenced by Brecht, whose major ideas had evolved out of experiences in the Weimar Republic. Like Brecht, Benjamin tried to develop the revolutionary tendencies of art out of the production relations of capitalism. His point of departure was the Marxist conviction that capitalism generates productive forces that make the abolition of capitalism both possible and necessary. For Benjamin, the productive forces in art are the artist himself and the artistic technique, especially the reproduction techniques used in film and photography. He acknowledges that it took much longer for the production relations of capitalistic society to make an impact on the superstructure than it took them to prevail at the basis, so much longer that they could only be analyzed in the 1930s.[39] From the very beginning of the essay on reproduction Benjamin insists upon the primacy of revolutionary movement at the basis. But the dialectics of the conditions of production leave their mark on the superstructure too. Recognizing this, Benjamin emphasizes the value of his theses as a weapon in the struggle for socialism. While Marcuse believes that the function of art will change *after* the social revolution, Benjamin sees change developing out of modern reproduction techniques, which drastically affect the inner structure of art. Here lies the importance of Benjamin for a materialist aesthetics still to be written.

Both essays by Benjamin make several references to Dada and cast a new light on the Pop debate. Benjamin found the "revolutionary strength of Dada"[40] in its testing of art for authenticity: by using new means of artistic production, the dadaists proved that this criterion of bourgeois aesthetics had become obsolete. In the reproduction essay Benjamin wrote "The dadaists attached much less importance to the sales value of their work than to its uselessness for contemplative immersion. The studied degradation of their material was not the least of their means to achieve this uselessness. Their poems are 'word salad' containing obscenities and every imaginable waste product of language. The same is true of their paintings, on which they mounted buttons and tickets. What they intended and achieved was a relentless destruction of the aura of their creations, which they branded as reproductions with the very means of production."[41] Benjamin recognized that Dada had been instrumental in destroying the bourgeois concept of an autonomous, genial, and eternal art. Contemplative immersion, which had been quite progressive in an earlier phase of bourgeois emancipation, since the late 19th century had served to sabotage any kind of social praxis geared toward change. During the decline of middle-class society, "contemplation became a school for asocial behavior."[42] It is the undeniable merit of the dadaists that they exposed this problem in their works. Benjamin did not overlook the fact that the Dada revolt was ultimately unsuccessful, however. He explored the reason for its failure in a 1929 essay on surrealism: "If it is the double task of the revolutionary intelligentsia to overthrow the intellectual predominance of the bourgeosie and to make contact with the proletarian masses, the intelligentsia has failed almost entirely in the second part of this task because it can no longer be performed contemplatively."[43] Out of negation alone, neither a new art nor a new society can be developed.

It was also Benjamin, of course, who praised John Heartfield for salvaging the revolutionary nature of Dada by incorporating its techniques into photomontage.[44] Heartfield, who like other leftist intellectuals (Grosz, Piscator) had joined the KPD in 1918, published his photomontages in such working class publications as *AIZ (Arbeiter Illustrierte Zeitung)* and *Volks-Illustrierte*.[45] He fulfilled two of Benjamin's major demands—the application and use of modern artistic techniques (photography and montage), and partisanship and active participation of the artist in the class struggle. For Benjamin, the key question was not the position of a work of art *vis-à-vis* the productive relations of its time, but rather its position *within* them.[46] Nor does Benjamin ask, what is the position of the artist *vis-à-vis* the production process, but rather, what is his position *within* it? The decisive passage in "The Author as Producer" reads: "Brecht has coined the phrase 'functional transformation' *(Umfunktionierung)* to describe the transformation of forms and instruments of production by a progressive intelligentsia—an intelligentsia interested in liberating the means of production and hence active in the class struggle. He was the first to address to the intellectuals the far-reaching demand that they should not supply the production apparatus without, at the same time, within the limits of the possible, changing that apparatus in the direction of Socialism."[47]

In opposition to Adorno, Benjamin held a positive view of modern reproduction techniques as they were applied in art. This disagreement can be traced to their respectively different understandings of capitalism, rooted in different experiences and formed at different times. To put it simply, Adorno was looking at the U.S. of the 1940s, Benjamin at the Soviet Union of the 1920s. Another important factor is that, like Brecht, Benjamin saw great potential in the "Americanism" introduced in Germany in the 1920s, while Adorno never overcame his deep mistrust of anything American. Both authors, however, have to be criticized for a distortion of perspective which makes it problematic to apply their theories in the 1970s. Just as we should question Adorno's view of the United States, we should be skeptical about Benjamin's idealizing enthusiasm for the early Soviet Union, which sometimes borders on a prolet-cult position. Neither Adorno's thesis of the total manipulation of culture (cf. his one-dimensional interpretation of jazz), nor Benjamin's absolute belief in the revolutionizing effects of modern reproduction techniques, has withstood the test of time. Benjamin, to be sure, was aware that mass production and mass reproduction in no way automatically guaranteed art an emancipatory function—not when art was subjected to the capitalist production and distribution apparatus. But it was not until Adorno that a theory of manipulated art under the capitalist culture industry was fully developed.

This leads us back to the Pop Art debate. According to Benjamin's theory, the artist, merely by seeing himself as producer and operating with the new reproduction techniques, would come closer to the proletariat. But this did not happen to the Pop artist, because the role that reproduction techniques play in today's art is totally different from what it was in the 1920s. At that time reproduction techniques called the bourgeois cultural tradition into question; today they confirm the myth of technological progress on all levels. And yet, modern reproduction techniques have a progressive potential even today. The technical innovation at the heart of Warhol's work is the use of photography combined with the silk screen technique. Because this technique makes the unlimited distribution of art works possible, it has the potential to assume a political function. Like film and photography, the silk screen destroys the century-old aura[48] of the work of art, which, according to Benjamin, is the prerequisite for its autonomy and authenticity. It is not surprising that in 1970 a Warhol monograph—using Benjamin and Brecht's categories—claimed that Warhol's opus was *the* new critical art of our times.[49] The author, Rainer Crone, was right to view the silk screen technique in the light of Benjamin's thesis that "to an ever greater degree the work of art reproduced becomes the work of art designed for reproducibility."[50] Warhol, Crone claimed, forces the observer to redefine the role of painting as a medium. One might object that such a redefinition already had been made necessary by Dada. There is a more important objection to be made, however. Crone's interpretation is based exclusively on an analysis of Warhol's artistic techniques; he completely ignores Benjamin's linking of artistic technique and political mass movement. Benjamin, who found his model in the revolutionary Russian film, wanted the bourgeois contemplative reception of art replaced by a collective reception.

Yet, when Pop Art is shown today in the Museum of Modern Art or in the Wallraf-Richartz-Museum in Cologne, the reception remains contemplative and thus Pop remains a form of autonomous bourgeois art. Crone's Warhol interpretation can only be regarded as a failure because he lifts Benjamin's theories out of their political context and neglects all the problems that would be posed by an application of those theories to today's art. A major contradiction of Crone's approach is that on the one hand, he supports Warhol's attack on the autonomy of art and the originality of the artist, and on the other hand, writes a book which glorifies the originality of Warhol and of his art. The aura absent from Warhol's works is thus reintroduced in a kind of star cult, in the "auratization" of the artist Andy Warhol.

In another context, however, Benjamin's theories can be related to Pop Art. Benjamin trusted in the capacity of revolutionary art to stimulate the needs of the masses and to turn into material force when those needs could only be satisfied by collective praxis. That Pop was seen as a critical art at the time of the anti-authoritarian protest cannot be understood if one adheres to the thesis that art equals commodity. Viewed from Benjamin's perspective, however, this interpretation was valid so long as the Pop reception was part of a political movement in the Federal Republic. We can also understand now that the interpretation of Pop as a progressive art had to change once the anti-authoritarian student movement foundered on its internal and external contradictions. By that time, of course, Pop had already been co-opted by the museums and collectors as the newest form of high art.

Toward a Transformation of Everyday Life

The views of Adorno and Benjamin are diametrically opposed, and neither offers totally satisfying solutions to today's problems. Adorno's thesis of total manipulation and his conclusion that serious art has to maintain an autonomy of negation must be refuted as well as the often naïve belief of Brecht and Benjamin that new artistic techniques might lead to an elimination of bourgeois culture. And yet, if Adorno's critique of the capitalist culture industry is combined with the theories of Brecht and Benjamin, it is still valid. Only from such a synthesis can we hope to develop a theory and praxis leading eventually to the integration of art into the material life process once called for by Marcuse. It does not make much sense to play one position against the other. It is more important to preserve that which can still be of use today—not only certain elements of theory, but also whatever was progressive in the Pop reception of the anti-authoritarian student movement and in the movement itself.

It seems to me that both artists and exhibitors have learned from the reception and critique of United States Pop Art. At a recent Documenta exhibit,[51] three tendencies could be observed. While the American photorealism continued to adhere closely to reproduced reality (thus drawing the same kind of criticism levelled at Pop Art earlier), the Concept artists almost completely withdrew from image into the cerebral. This withdrawal from the reality of pictorial presentation can be interpreted as a reaction against the oversaturation of our consciousness with reproduced images, or as an expression of the problem that in our world many crucial experiences are no longer sensuous and concrete. At the same time, however, Concept art perpetuates the suppression of sensuousness so characteristic of contemporary capitalist society. It seems to lead back into the vicious circle of abstraction and coldness in which Adrian Leverkühn was trapped. The reduction of the traditionally aesthetic[52] has reached a point where the work no longer communicates with the audience because there is no concrete work left. Here modernism has pursued its course to a logical extreme.

More interesting results of Pop came to light in another area of the Documenta, particularly in the documentation of the imagery of daily life which was taken seriously for the first time. Cover pages of the newsweekly *Der Spiegel* were exhibited along with trivial emblems, garden dwarfs, votive pictures, ads, and political posters. A widely publicized show in Düsseldorf had a similar intent. Its theme was the eagle as a sign or symbol. The close relationship to Jasper Johns's flag canvases is obvious.

In 1974 the Berlin Academy of Art presented a documentary show called *Die Strasse* in which photographs and maps of city cultures from around the world were related directly to Berlin's urban renewal plans. Such shows, especially the last one, aim not only at an interpretation of daily life but also at its transformation.

If Pop Art has drawn our attention to the imagery of daily life, demanding that the separation of high and low art be eliminated, then today it is the task of the artist to break out of art's ivory tower and contribute to a change of everyday life. He would be following the precepts of Henri Lefebvre's *La vie quotidienne dans le monde moderne (Daily Life in the Mod-*

71

ern World), no longer accepting the separation of the philosophical and the non-philosophical, the high and the low, the spiritual and the material, the theoretical and the practical, the cultivated and the non-cultivated; and not planning only a change of the state, of political life, economic production and judicial and social structures, but also planning a change of everyday life.[53] Aesthetics should not be forgotten in such attempts to change everyday life. The aesthetic activity of human beings not only manifests itself in the iconic arts but in all spheres of human activity. Marx wrote: "An animal forms things in accordance with the measure and the need of the species to which it belongs, while man knows how to produce in accordance with the measure of every species and knows how to apply everywhere the inherent measure to the object. Man, therefore, also forms things in accordance with the laws of beauty."[54] Along with Marx we must understand the transformation of everyday life as "practical human-sensuous activity,"[55] an activity that must enter into all spheres of human production—the forming of nature and cities, of home and work place, of traffic systems and vehicles, of clothing and instruments, body and movement. This does not mean that all differences between art and daily life should be eliminated. In a liberated human society there would be art *qua* art as well. Today more than ever it is the task of Marxist critics to expose the popular equation of art and life for what it is—nothing but a mystification; what we need is a critical analysis of the unprecedented aesthetization of everyday life that took place in Western countries in the postwar era. While Pop Art disclosed the commodity character of art, the Federal Republic witnessed an aesthetization of commodities (including advertising and window displays) which totally subjugated the aesthetic to the interest of capital.[56] Remembering Marx's thesis that the human senses are the result of thousands of years of development, we may legitimately ask whether human sensuality itself might not undergo a qualitative change if the present manipulation of our sense perceptions is continued over a long period of time. A Marxist theory of sensuality and fantasy under late capitalism must be developed, and this theory should provide an impulse to change everyday life. Even false, crippled needs are needs and—as Ernst Bloch has shown—contain a kernel of human dream, hope, and concrete utopia. In the context of the student movement in the Federal Republic, Pop Art succeeded in evoking progressive needs. Today the goal still should be a functional transformation (*Umfunktionierung*) of false needs in an attempt to change everyday life. In the Paris manuscripts, Marx predicted that the human senses would be liberated as a result of the elimination of private property. We know today that the elimination of private property is at most a necessary condition, but not a sufficient cause for the emancipation of human sensuality. On the other hand, the Pop reception in the Federal Republic has shown that even in capitalism there can arise forces which insist on overcoming the suppression of sensuality, and thus challenge the capitalist system as a whole. To understand and utilize such forces—that is the task at hand.

Notes:

1) See Jost Hermand, *Pop International* (Frankfurt am Main: Athenäum, 1971), pp. 47-51.

2) In the early 1960s there were less than a thousand galleries in the FRG: in 1970 the number of galleries had more than doubled. See Gottfried Sello, "Blick zurück im Luxus," *Die Zeit*, 44 (November 1, 1974), 9.

3) See Hermand, *Pop International*, p. 14; Jürgen Wissmann, "Pop Art oder die Realität als Kunstwerk," *Die nicht mehr schönen Künste*, ed. H.R. Jauss (Munich: Wilhelm Fink, 1968), pp. 507-530.

4) Alan R. Solomon, "The New Art," *Art International*, 7 : 1 (1963), 37.

5) Thomas Mann, *Doctor Faustus*, Trans. H.T. Lowe-Porter (New York: Alfred A. Knopf, 1948), p. 238 f.

6) Ibid., p. 240.

7) Theodor W. Adorno and Max Horkheimer, *Dialectic of Enlightenment*. trans. John Cumming (New York: Herder & Herder, 1972).

8) Theodor W. Adorno, "Résumé über die Kulturindustrie," *Ohne Leitbild* (Frankfurt am Main: Suhrkamp, 1967), p. 60. American translation "Culture Industry Reconsidered," *New German Critique*, 6 (Fall 1975), 12-19.

9) Herbert Marcuse, "The Affirmative Character of Culture," *Negations: Essays in Critical Theory* (Boston: Beacon Press, 1968), p. 114.

10) Ibid., p. 131.

11) Jürgen Habermas, "Bewusstmachende oder rettende Kritik—die Aktualität Walter Benjamins," *Zur Aktualität Walter Benjamins* (Frankfurt am Main: Suhrkamp, 1972), p. 178 f. American translation "Consciousness-Raising or Redemptive Criticism: The Contemporaneity of Walter Benjamin." *New German Critique*. 17 (Spring 1979), 30-59.

12) See Herbert Marcuse, *An Essay on Liberation* (Boston: Beacon Press, 1969); later, of course, Marcuse differentiated and modified his theses on the basis of new developments within the student revolt, underground and counter-culture: see Herbert Marcuse, *Counterrevolution and Revolt* (Boston: Beacon Press, 1972).

13) This is so even though again and again there are critics who do not count Warhol among the Pop artists but see him as a genius *sui generis*.

14) For a description of Warhol's silk screen technique see Rainer Crone, *Andy Warhol* (New York: Praeger, 1970). p. 11.

15) In April 1974, the real *Mona Lisa* was carried in procession from the Louvre to Japan and was exhibited there rather as a stimulus to French national pride and

Japanese business (cf. *Newsweek*, May 6, 1974, 44) than as a genuine attempt to take the masterpiece to the masses.

16) Cf. Catalogue of the Marcel Duchamp exhibit, edited by Anne d'Harnoncourt and Kynaston McShine (New York, 1973).

17) For a more elaborate interpretation of this work see Max Imdahl, "Vier Aspekte zum Problem der ästhetischen Grenzüberschreitung in der bilden Kunst," *Die nicht mehr schönen Künste*, ed. H.R. Jauss (Munich: Wilhelm Fink, 1968), p. 494.

18) Ibid., p. 494.

19) The playing card Mona Lisa was exhibited at the latest Duchamp exhibit in New York (1973) and Chicago (1974).

20) See Hartmut Scheible, "Wow, das Yoghurt ist gut," *Frankfurter Hefte*, 27:11 (1972), 817-824.

21) Reprinted in John Russell and Suzi Gablik, *Pop Art Redefined* (New York: Praeger, 1969), p. 116.

22) See the essays collected and edited by Hermann K. Ehmer, *Visuelle Kommunikation: Beiträge zur Kritik der Bewusstseinsindustrie* (Cologne: Dumont, 1971) and Hermand, *Pop International*.

23) One might theorize that critical interest in comics as a form of popular culture is not unrelated to Lichtenstein's introduction of comics into the realm of high art.

24) See the essays by Heino R. Möller, Hans Roosen and Herman K. Ehmer in *Visuelle Kommunikation* for further discussion of the relationship between Pop and advertising.

25) Interview conducted by G.R. Swenson. Reprinted in Russell and Gablik, *Pop Art Redefined*, p. 111.

26) Cf. Hermand, *Pop International*, p. 50 f.

27) *Kursbuch*, 15 (November, 1968): *Die Zeit*, 48 (November 29, 1968), 22.

28) Ibid.

29) Karl Markus Michel, "Ein Kranz für die Literatur," *Kursbuch*, 15 (November, 1968), 177.

30) Hans Magnus Enzensberger, "Gemeinplätze, die Neueste Literatur betreffend," *Kursbuch*, 15 (November, 1968), 190.

31) Ibid., 195.

32) Ibid., 197.

33) This presentation of Enzensberger's position limits itself to the 1968 *Kursbuch* article. It neither deals with his earlier ideas nor with his later development, which would go beyond the scope of the problems under consideration in this article.

34) Ibid., 188.

35) This is not to deny that frequently the distribution apparatus has a direct impact on artistic production itself.

36) Walter Benjamin, "The Author as Producer," *Understanding Brecht*, trans. Anna Bostock (London: New Left Books, 1973), p. 94.

37) The debate took place in *Das Argument*, 46 (March, 1968), *Alternative*, 56/57 *(October/December 1967)*, and 59/60 *(April/June, 1968)*, *Merkur*, 3 (1967) and 1-2 (1968), and *Frankfurter Rundschau*. For a detailed bibliography see *Alternative*, 59/60 (April/June, 1968), 93.

38) For differences between Benjamin and Marcuse see Habermas, "Bewusstmachende oder rettende Kritik," pp. 177-185.

39) Walter Benjamin, "The Work of Art in the Age of Mechanical Reproduction," in *Illuminations*, ed. by Hannah Arendt, trans. Harry Zohn (New York: Schocken Books, 1969), p. 217 f.

40) Benjamin, "Author as Producer," p. 94.

41) Ibid., p. 296.

42) Ibid.

43) Walter Benjamin, "Surrealism," in *Reflections*, ed. by Peter Demetz, trans. Edmond Jephcott (New York & London: Harcourt Brace Jovanovich, 1978) p. 191.

44) Benjamin, "Author as Producer," p. 94.

45) See the first book of Heartfield's work published in the Federal Republic; John Heartfield, *Krieg im Frieden* (Munich: Hanser, 1972).

46) Ibid., p. 87.

47) Ibid., p. 93.

48) For an explanation of Benjamin's notion of aura see Habermas, "Bewusstmachende oder rettende Kritik," Michael Scharang, *Zur Emanzipation der Kunst* (Neuwied: Luchterhand, 1971), pp. 7-25, Lienhard Wawrzyn, *Walter Benjamins Kunsttheorie, Kritik einer Rezeption* (Neuwied: Luchterhand, 1973), especially pp. 25-39.

49) Crone, *Andy Warhol*, op. cit.

50) Benjamin, "Mechanical Reproduction," p. 224.

51) *Documenta V*. Kassel 1972.

52) Hans Dieter Junker, "Die Reduktion der ästhetischen Struktur—Ein Aspekt der Kunst der Gegenwart," *Visuelle Kommunikation*. pp. 9-58.

53) See Henri Lefebvre, *Das Alltagsleben in der modernen Welt* (Frankfurt am Main: Suhrkamp, 1972), p. 26.

54) Karl Marx, *Economic and Philosophic Manuscripts of 1844.* Quoted from Marx and Engels, *On Literature and Art,* ed. Lee Baxandall and Stefan Morawski (St. Louis and Milwaukee, 1973) p. 51.

55) Karl Marx, *Theses on Feuerbach* (thesis 5).

56) For a discussion of commodity aesthetics see Wolfgang Fritz Haug, *Kritik der Warenästhetik* (Frankfurt am Main: Suhrkamp, 1971), and Lutz Holzinger, *Der produzierte Mangel* (Starnberg: Raith Verlag, 1973).

IN POOR TASTE
DICK HEBDIGE

Pop was meant as a cultural break, signifying the firing squad without mercy or reprieve, for the kind of people who believed in the Loeb classics, holidays in Tuscany, drawings by Augustus John, signed pieces of French furniture, leading articles in the Daily Telegraph and very good clothes that lasted forever . . . (Reyner Banham)

One thing I dislike more than being taken too lightly is being taken too seriously. (Billy Wilder)

David Hockney painted *Two Boys Together Clinging* in 1959. It exhibits many of the qualities characteristic of Hockney's later work—a self-consciously deployed pictorial naïveté which is contradicted by the accomplished and painterly manner in which that naïveté is communicated . . . hence subverted . . . and there is the reference to homosexual love: two boys and a black heart in the left hand corner. There is nothing particularly "Pop" about it. It comes as some surprise, then, to learn the apparent source of inspiration. For, like the earlier Hockney painting, *Doll Boy*—a reference to the record, *(Got Myself) a Walking, Talking Living Doll*—this painting was originally suggested, according to the artist's own account, by a chance association with Cliff Richards . . .

According to the catalogue *Pop Art in England*, produced in 1976 for the York City Gallery and translated somewhat awkwardly from the original German, Hockney was partly inspired by a line from a Walt Whitman poem. But what clinched the painting (and its title) was a newspaper headline which had caught Hockney's eye. It read TWO BOYS CLING TO CLIFF ALL NIGHT:

> *. . . at first glance, Hockney had thought that this meant Cliff Richards, to whom at that time he felt himself very strongly drawn; but it actually referred to a cliff.*[1]

The apparently chance association with what was then regarded in fine art circles as the netherworld of popular music and the laconic, deadpan manner in which Hockney "explains" the reference and the painting are pure Pop. The canvas has been polluted not by the homosexual allusions— homoerotic art was, even in the '50s, within limits permissible—as old as ancient Greece, as old, at least, as the Yellow Book. But the incorporation of ersatz motifs drawn from commercial Pop culture represented a new turn of the screw in the art of "épater les bourgeois."

Pop Art and Pop art critics were drenched in the rhetoric of the most despised forms of popular culture. They used the most soiled and damaged currency. This is how Richard Smith, writing in the Royal College's house journal, *Ark,* in 1960 described David Hockney's *curtain of fantasy:*

(It is) as essential as Bardot's towel. Hockney's range may be narrow as the lapels on his jacket but within his terms, he has made a highly successful, personalized statement . . .[2]

The logic of this analogy is immaterial. What matters is the style of the review, the references to fashion, to the forbidden ephemera, to the details and the dress. That is what counts, together with the implication secreted within it, that the traditional hierarchical ranking of art and design—a ranking established during the Renaissance—moving down in descending order of merit, importance and spiritual value from fine art through graphics to the decorative arts—has been overthrown and cast aside. And with this, another implication—that the disruption of established formal values signals the collapse not only of aesthetic boundaries but of the principle of exclusivity—of social segregation—which those boundaries are erected to maintain: the return (yet again) of the repressed. Art's sacred vessel seized by a gang of low-born pirates. This implication is echoed four years later by Jonathan Miller writing in *The New Statesman*:

There is now a curious cultural community, breathlessly à la Mod where Lord Snowdon and the other desperadoes of the grainy layout jostle with commercial art-school Mersey stars, window dressers and Carnaby Street pants-peddlers. Style is the thing here—Taste 64—a cool line and the witty insolence of youth.[3]

A similar convergence of previously segregated social types occurs in New York at around the same time. A bright, brittle ambiance was created in the lofts and galleries of

Manhattan in which fashion, fine art, photography and film provided a platform for a new kind of cultural entrepreneur: the artist-as-star.

The rise of Pop Art in New York was associated with the emergence of a *nouveau riche* art market—socially ambitious, upwardly mobile, epitomized by Tom Wolfe in the person of Robert C. Scull, former cab-driver turned executive and Pop Art collector. Scull, the man who bought Jasper Johns's beer cans from Leo Castelli in 1965 and who was the subject of one of Wolfe's cruellest and most telling cameos, an essay which originally appeared in *New York* magazine under the title *Upward with the Arts.*

Bob Scull, the man whose motto was *Enjoy, Enjoy,* the man who walked into a Savile Row tailors when on a trip to London and ordered, in the face of frosty Anglo-Saxon opposition, a sports jacket in traditional riding pink. Tom Wolfe describes the first fitting a week later:

... they bring out the riding pink, with the body of the coat cut and basted up and one arm basted on, the usual first fitting, and they put it on him—and Scull notices a funny thing. Everything has stopped in the shop. There, in the dimness of the woodwork and bolt racks, the other men are looking up towards him, and in the back, from behind the curtains, around door edges, from behind tiers of cloth, are all these eyes, staring.
Scull motions back toward all the eyes and asks his man, "Hey, what are they doing?"
The man leans forward and says, very softly and very sincerely, "They're rooting for you, sir."
Enjoy! Enjoy![4]

And yet, Sidney Tillim writing in *Artforum* in 1965 could say:

The pop art audience, as arrogant and arriviste as much of it is, is involved with art in a way that I think no American art public has been involved before. It is concerned less with art, with quality than with the release of a spirit that has been repressed by its subservience to an idea of culture essentially foreign to its audience. The pop audience is tired of being educated, tired of merely good art.[5]

Pop clearly forms part of that quest for an American vernacular in which European pictorial conventions are seen to re-present, however obliquely, a rigid and alien social structure, a hierarchy of taste, which is essentially European, where "taste" functions as a marker between the social classes, where "good taste" is inscribed above a door which is reserved for "Members Only."

Mark Twain had stood outside that door a hundred years earlier when, in 1867, he boarded the ship *Quarter City* for the very first American package tour of Europe. In Italy, as the first of Scott Fitzgerald's *fantastic neanderthals,* he *suffered* the ruins, the art works and the gondoliers and when he returned home he wrote:

I never felt so fervently thankful, so soothed, so tranquil, so filled with blessed peace as I did yesterday when I learned that Michelangelo was dead.[6]

In Pop—in the figure of Bob C. Scull—Mark Twain and America finally had their revenge on Europe.

This is undoubtedly familiar territory: part of Pop's copious folklore. Pop's contribution to "cultural politics" lies precisely in the manner in which it served to problematize those two terms, "culture" and "politics", by abandoning the tone (of solemnity, of 'seriousness') in which any "radical" proposal in bourgeois art and art criticism—avant-garde or otherwise—is conventionally presented. The brief glances above at London and New York Pop in the '60s encapsulate its themes:

(i) what might be described as Pop's deictic function—the way in which it can be used to point up the complicity between aesthetic taste, and economic and symbolic power.

(ii) Pop as an inspired move in the Culture Game, the object of which is to fix the shifting line between "sensation" and "spirit", "low" and "high", "art" and "non-art"—categories which Pierre Bourdieu has shown to be co-terminous.

(iii) Pop Art as a strategy in another "taste war" (the same war, in fact, fought along a different front) between the Old and New Worlds, between an America which, as Leslie Fiedler puts it, *has had to be invented as well as discovered* and a Europe with its long literary and aesthetic traditions, its complex codings of class and status—between, that is, two continents and a history, between two symbolic blocs: "Europe" and "America."

(iv) Finally, less grandly but no less seriously, Pop as a discourse on fashion, consumption and fine art; Pop as a discourse on what Lawrence Alloway called, in 1959, "the drama of possessions."[7] Pop as a new suit of clothes: a sports jacket in riding pink with narrow lapels.

The emphasis here will fall mainly on British Pop though

comparisons will be drawn wherever these are relevant with the work of American Pop artists and the critical reception Pop Art received in the States. The development of British Pop Art falls into three approximate phases. The first is associated with the work of the Independent Group at the ICA and spans the years 1952-55. This is generally understood as the period of Pop's underground gestation during which the members of the Group and most especially Eduardo Paolozzi and Richard Hamilton developed many of the obsessional motifs and representational techniques which were later to surface to such sensational effect though in a slightly different form within the Royal College of Art during the second and third phases. The second phase is usually dated from 1957-59 and is associated with the early work of Peter Blake and Richard Smith.

The third stage during which British Pop is seen to emerge as a distinct, more or less coherent "movement" (though it is often conceded that Pop was in fact, never much more than an ad hoc grouping of Young Contemporaries) is generally held to incorporate at least some of the early work of Derek Boshier, Patrick Caulfield, David Hockney, Allen Jones, Ronald Kitaj and Peter Philips. It was during this phase that Pop attracted an enormous amount of publicity, thanks partly to the exposure afforded by the annual Young Contemporaries exhibitions and by the Ken Russell TV documentary *Pop Goes the Easel* which was broadcast in 1962 and which helped to establish the stereotype of the young, iconoclastic and highly sexed male Pop artist whose "lifestyle," to use another '60s keyword, was conspicuously in the Swinging London mode. The program also helped to fix Pop Art in the public imagination as the corollary in the visual arts to the British beat and fashion booms which were beginning to gather a similar momentum at about the same time.

By the mid-'60s, the word "Pop," like its sister words "mod," "beat" and "permissive," had become so thoroughly devalued by over-usage that it tended to serve as a kind of loose, linguistic genuflexion made ritualistically by members of the Press towards work that was vaguely contemporary in tone and/or figurative in manner, that leant heavily towards the primary end of the color range and which could be linked—however tenuously—to the "swinging" milieu.

The one thing everyone hated was commercial art; apparently they didn't hate that enough either. (Roy Lichtenstein)

Pop Art in Britain has become thoroughly absorbed into the language of commercial art and packaging—dictating, for instance, the peculiarly ironic tone of so much "quality" British advertising—that we are in danger of losing sight of the radical nature of its original proposal: that popular culture and mass-produced imagery are worthy of consideration *in their own right* and in addition *almost incidentally* provide a rich iconographical resource to be tapped by those working within the fine arts. It is easy to forget, for instance, that when it first appeared in this country in the 1950s, Pop presented itself and was widely construed in critical circles as a form of symbolic aggression and that it fell into an awkward, unexplored space somewhere between fine art and graphics, between, that is— to use the critical oppositions of the time—on the one hand, fine art: the validated, the creative, the pure; and on the other, graphics: the despicable, the commercial, the compromised. The assumed incompatibility of art and commerce is clearly registered in some of the protests which greeted Pop's emergence. For instance, in an article entitled *Anti-Sensibility Painting* which appeared in *Artforum*, in 1963, Ivan Karp wrote:

The formulations of the commercial artist are deeply antagonistic to the fine arts. In his manipulation of significant form, the tricky commercial conventions accrue. These conventions are a despoliation of inspired invention . . .[8]

During the late '50s and early '60s, the arts field was still being scanned continuously by self-appointed defenders of "good taste," determined to "maintain standards." Points of potential "cross over" and "breakdown" were particularly susceptible to this kind of monitoring. Trespassers could be prosecuted. When Janey Ironside, using William Morris wallpaper blocks, transferred the bold designs to her textiles in 1960, the William Morris Society lodged a complaint with the Royal College authorities.[9] As the prolonged austerity of the '40s and early '50s gave way to a period of relative affluence, the official tastemaking bodies sought new ways to extend their paternalistic influence over popular tastes. The BBC, presumably in an attempt to arrest the cultural decline with which commercial television was commonly equated amongst the BBC hierarchy, set out to "educate" the new consumers. According to John McHale:

(There was) a calculated co-operation between the BBC and the

*Council for Industrial Design . . . Around mid-1956, a fire was
written into the script of The Grove Family television series—so
that the "family" could refurnish their "home" through the Design
Centre.*[10]

Pop challenged the legitimacy of validated distinctions
between the arts and the lingering authority of pre-War taste
formations. The "lessons" inscribed in Pop's chosen objects—
Americana, "slick graphics," pop music, etc.—matched BBC
didacticism point for point and turned it upside down. Where
the BBC counselled discrimination and sobriety, Pop recommended excess and aspiration.

Clearly the emergence of the new visual sensibility that
found its expression in Pop is linked to the shift in the social
composition of the Art Schools during the '50s. It is often
claimed that Pop embodied the aspirations of a new generation of art students—many from working class or lower
middle class backgrounds, the first beneficiaries in the immediate post-War period of servicemen's grants and the 1944
Butler Education Act. Pop, in Reyner Banham's words,
represented *the revenge of the elementary schoolboys.* Also
(and this is no coincidence) it augured the revenge of graphics
on fine art. Pop was just the first, most visible sign of the move
within art education after the War away from the craft-based
disciplines towards a more direct engagement with a profes-
sional design and the needs of industry. (The Coldstream
Council submitted its recommendations for the expansion of
design within art education in 1957). The break with tradition
was first signaled by a symbolic defection on the part of some
British artists, architects and art students to the forbidden,

glossy continent of American graphic and product design. Banham, writing in 1969 described that defection:

. . . it is important to realize how salutary a corrective to the sloppy provincialism of most London art ten years ago, American design could be. The gusto and professionalism of widescreen movies or Detroit car styling was a constant reproach to the Mooreish yokelry of British sculpture, or the affected Piperish gloom of British painting. To anyone with a scrap of sensibility or an eye to technique, the average Playtex or Maidenform ad in American Vogue *was an instant deflater of most artists then in Arts Council vogue.*[11]

It is then, easy to overlook that when Pop first appeared, it was both orphan and bastard and was, in the very early days stigmatized accordingly. The fact that it was subsequently adopted, redeemed, lifted up and transformed—rather in the manner of Dickens' protagonist in the last chapter of *Oliver Twist*: lost aristocratic lineage suddenly revealed, vast fortunes suddenly inherited—the fact that this miraculous redemption did occur, is, in this context, neither here nor there.

Pop also tends to fare so badly, or at least indifferently, within the existing canons of Art History, is so consistently rejected, disapproved of or condoned with strong reservations, that one begins to wonder what else is at stake. Pop tends to be reified within art history as a particular moment, a distinct school of painting, sculpture and print-making which falls within a discrete historical period, i.e. roughly from '53 to '69, and is defined simply as that-which-was-exhibited-as-Pop.

Alternatively, Pop is interpreted as a kind of internal *putsch,* as a reaction occurring more or less exclusively within the confines of the art world. From this viewpoint, Pop is regarded as a more or less conscious move on the part of a group of ambitious young Turks, intent on displacing an older group of already established Academy painters and sculptors—in Britain, Henry Moore, Stanley Spencer, Graham Sutherland et al; in the U.S., Jackson Pollock and the Abstract Expressionists. Here Pop is conceived of as a struggle conducted at the point where the Art Game meets the Generation Game. Or—and this is a slight variation—Pop is seen as a term in a more general dialectic of pictorial styles—a dialectic which, in the late '50s, clearly dictated a move away from what was already there: abstraction and "kitchen sink realism": the work of John Bratby, Jack Smith, Edward Middleditch etc. As Robert Indiana put it in 1963, *Pop is everything art hasn't been for the last two decades.*[12]

There is some truth in both these interpretations. As Bourdieu points out, in order to create value and recognition in the art world, one must first create a *difference*. This, after all, provides the economic logic which governs most areas of cultural production. It is this logic which generates both change and small change within the art world, which creates the *value* (in both senses) of the art object and which also determines the literally outrageous form of so much avant-garde practice.

However, neither of these definitions permits an analysis of the extraordinary effectivity of Pop as a visual idiom *outside* fine art; the sheer variety of poster and print making—which Pop helped to get consecrated as fine art. In other words, both definitions inhibit an investigation of Pop's wider cultural currency. I would argue that the significance of Pop lies elsewhere, beyond the scope of traditional art history, in the way in which it posed questions about the relationship between culture in its classical-conservative sense—culture as, in Matthew Arnold's words, *the best that has been thought and said in the world*—and culture in its anthropological sense: culture as the distinctive patterns, rituals and expressive forms which together constitute the "whole way of life" of a community or social group.

We should remember, for instance, that the word "Pop" was originally coined by Lawrence Alloway and was used to refer not to the collages, prints and later paintings produced by Hamilton and Paolozzi but rather to the raw material for both these artists' work—the ads, comics, posters, packages, etc.— the scraps and traces of Americana which had been smuggled into the country by GI's, enterprising stationers and John McHale—scraps and traces which spoke of yet another more affluent, more attractive popular culture which had, in the early '50s, yet to be properly established in Great Britain. The term, "Pop," then, is itself riddled with ambiguity. It stands poised somewhere between the Independent Group's (IG) present and some imagined future, between their artistic aspirations and their experience of cultural deprivation in Britain in the early '50s. And the early work of Paolozzi and the IG presentations and exhibitons—*Parallels of Life and Art* (1953), *Objects and Collages* (1954), and *This is Tomorrow* (1956) were motivated by a common pledge not only to produce a new kind of visual environment but also to analyze critically the fabric of everyday life and mass produced imagery.

It should also be recalled that the tone of the early IG

91

meetings at the ICA was self-consciously pitched towards a consideration of science and engineering rather than art, that cybernetics, Detroit car styling and helicopter design figured amongst the early topics of discussion at those meetings, that Paolozzi professed a marked preference for science museums over art galleries, that he later wrote about the origins of Pop that *there were other valid considerations about art beside the aesthetic ones, basically sociological, anthropological . . .*[13] It should be remembered, too, that as early as 1959 Alloway was arguing for the development of a sociologically-inflected, "audience-oriented model for understanding mass art"[14]—the beginnings of a reception-aesthetic which would seek to account for the variable significance of objects and images as they circulated in different consumer markets. In other words, Pop formed up at the interface between the analysis of "popular culture" and the production of "art," on the turning point between those two opposing definitions of culture: culture as a standard of excellence, culture as a descriptive category. The questions Pop Art poses simply cannot be answered within the narrowly art historical framework which most of the critical research on Pop Art seems to inhabit.

Here, we are beginning to touch on what I hinted at earlier: that there are larger issues at stake here in the silences and antipathies which surround Pop in critical and art historical discourse. For there is a third position on Pop, a position which we find uniting critics who would normally find little common ground in terms either of ideology or aesthetics—critics as dissimilar as, on the one hand, Clement Greenberg and John Canaday, the conservative reviewer on *The New York Times* at the height of U.S. Pop, and, on the other, Peter

Fuller and Hugh Adams, author of the comparatively recent retrospective, *Art in the Sixties*.

This unlikely consensus is formed around the shared perception that whatever else Pop Art was or wasn't, it certainly wasn't *serious* enough.

What rendered Pop suspect for both radicals and traditionalists was its instant commercial success in the art market—i.e., in relative terms, its popularity—and these suspicions have been reinforced by the ease with which Pop Art techniques have been incorporated into the persuasive strategies deployed by the advertising industry.

Canaday dubbed Pop "a commercial hype" which resolved the crisis facing American art critics and dealers during the late '50s when the market was inundated with mundane examples of Abstract Expressionism. In this situation, the appearance of Pop was "equivalent to the discovery of a critical Klondike."[15] Irving Sandler, writing in the *New York Post* in 1962, suggested that Pop was receiving an inordinate amount of unjustified exposure in what he called the "slick magazines" because it served to authorize and render respectable the advertising ethos which informs the "commercial end" of the publishing business.[16] Amongst the radical camp, Pop tends to be condemned for its complicity in the Art Game because of its unquestioning commitment to the gallery system and the bourgeois notion of the art object. Peter Fuller throws doubts on the achievements of Pop artists because "they failed to transcend the prevalent illusions of the late 1950s and the early '60s, the ideology of the affluent society."[17] Hugh Adams has argued that "any compelling ideas" communicated in Pop were:

so filtered by exploitative structures that they were diluted and debased to the point where . . . [They tended to degenerate into] . . . mere mindless Pop image peddlings.[18]

Similar objections to Pop's immoral flirtation with the worlds of commerce and fashion have been voiced by Lynda Morris—the pejorative tone of her article announced in its title, *What Made the Sixties' Art So Successful, So Shallow?*[19]

All these critics seem to concur in the opinion that Pop Art was a temporary aberration from the proper concerns of responsible artists, a silly, wrong-headed or empty-headed, essentially callow or immoral digression from the serious business of making serious statements—the business which these critics imply should preoccupy committed artists of whatever persuasion—academics, formalists, propagandists and populists alike. Against this I argue that that dismissive critical response merely reproduces unaltered the ideological distinction between, on the one hand, the "serious," the "artistic," the "political" and on the other, the "ephemeral," the "commercial," the "pleasurable,"—a set of distinctions which Pop Art itself exposed as being, at the very least, open to question, distinctions which Pop practice set out to erode. I argue that Pop's significance resides in the ways in which it demonstrated, illuminated, lit up in neon, the "loaded arbitrariness" of those parallel distinctions, lit up the hidden economy which serves to valorize certain objects, certain forms of expression, certain voices to the exclusion of other objects, other forms, other voices by bestowing upon them the mantle of Art.

I shall attempt to do this by isolating two moments in the

development of British Pop—in terms of my original chronology, the first and final phases—in order to invoke some of the themes and meanings which collected around it during the mid '50s and the mid to late '60s. The manner in which these two moments will be considered could be most accurately described as "invocation." This term is used to alert the reader to the fact that what follows is neither a simple chronological account of what happened, nor an overview in the conventional sense. I hope that the kind of flexibility and arbitrary detail which a word like "invocation" licenses will enable me to locate Pop within a broad cultural context, and will permit me (i) to propose some general connections which would be suppressed if a more sober presentation of the facts were attempted, (ii) to isolate the "taste problematic" which operates around Pop and the critical responses to it, and (iii) to summon up, like a medium at a seance, a medium in a message parlor, some of the peculiar connotative power which collected round the phrases "Pop Art" and "Pop artist" during the '50s and '60s.

It is difficult to recapture the austere visual and cultural context within which or rather against which British Pop first emerged in the early '50s. The documents and recollections which have filtered down from IG meetings stress the sheer lack of visual stimulation which afflicted every aspect of daily life in Britain at the time. The paucity of visual material merely underlined the shortage of goods. Rationing was not fully lifted till 1954. Packaging was virtually non-existent.

Against this were counterposed the exotic hyperboles of American design.

These images and objects function in Paolozzi's Scrap

Books as signs of freedom asserted against the economic and cultural constraints, as dreams, implicitly subversive "ready-made metaphors."[20]

I have argued elsewhere[21] that these signifiers were widely interpreted within the critical discourses of art and design and the broader streams of concerned, "responsible" commentary as harbingers of cultural decadence and the feminization of native traditions of discipline and self denial.

One example will suffice here. In an article which appeared in *Design* in 1959,[22] John Blake surveyed examples of contemporary product design for traces of American influence contrasting the "restraint and delicacy" of the tasteful European Mercedes air vent with the "heavy, over realistic" transposition of aircraft motifs to the air vent of the 1957 Pontiac. This curiously arbitrary logic—a perverted relic of the old modernist axiom that form should follow function—leads the author to conclude that the Italian-designed Lincoln Mercury is preferable to the vulgar and bulbous forms of the U.S. Cadillac on the grounds that the former presents a more "honest," more complete transplantation of aeroplane motifs.

These hysterical constructions of America as "enemy" were eventually to produce an "America" which could function for British Pop artists in the '50s (as the unconscious had for the surrealists in the '30s and '40s) as a repressed, potentially fertile realm invoked against the grain. Early Pop imagery drew its transgressive power from the friction generated in the clash between "official" and "unofficial" taste formations—a productive clash of opposing forces. The dialectic which gave Pop its difference can be presented through a series of juxtapositions:

Negative/official: Richard Hoggart intended to clinch his denunciation of cheap gangster fiction through the following analogy: *The authors are usually American or pseudo-American, after the manner of the American shirt-shops in the Charing Cross Road.*[23]

Positive/transgressive: Richard Hamilton, resorting to the cool mode, played back the language of the U.S. menswear ads.

Negative/official: Hoggart railed against the influence of Hollywood films on the "juke box boys." *They waggle one shoulder,* he wrote, *as desperately as Humphrey Bogart . . . across the tubular chairs.*[29]

Positive/transgressive: Alloway wrote approvingly in 1959 of the American cinema's, *lessons in style (of clothes, of bearing) . . . Films dealing with American home-life, such as the brilliant women's films from Universal-International, are in a similar way, lessons in the acquisition of objects, models for luxury, diagrams of bedroom arrangement.*[25]

Negative/official: Hoggart wrote that, *working people are exchanging their birthright for a mass of pin-ups.*[26]

Positive/transgressive: Peter Blake poses above a locker strewn with pin-ups.

Pop Art drew its power, then, from underneath the authorized discourses of good taste and good design. Pop artists dressed up, like the teddy boys, in the anxieties of the period. They converted their youth and their appropriation of "America" into future-threat.

The *content* of Tomorrow counted. The fact that Hamilton's *Hommage à Chrysler* used four different pictorial conventions to depict the shine on chromium was less important than the fact that the chromium of a Chrysler got depicted at all.

The *form* of Tomorrow counted: the blasphemy of reproduction. Screenprints, cut ups, photographs from magazines, epidiascopes: the promiscuity of collage which pointedly suggested that the craft-based tradition of the artist as sole point of creation was being superceded by the techniques of mass production and mass reproduction, that, just as the national identity was about to drown in the welter of imported, popular culture, so British painting was about to sink beneath a flood of anonymous, mass produced images.

By reconstructing the field of opposing forces, groups, tendencies and taste formations on which early British Pop was posited, one can begin to see the points at which its breaks and transgressions became meaningful and, in a strictly limited sense, progressive. This kind of mapping indicates, if nothing else, the provisional, historically located nature of any radical proposal within art. Such "radicalism" is conditional and contingent upon a number of historical givens—the availability or non-availability, the appropriateness or inappropriateness of different kinds of oppositional discourse. Criticisms of the aggressive fetishization and sexualization of women in Pop Art, at least during this period, or those blanket dismissals of Pop which take as their starting point the extent of American cultural and economic penetration of Britain's leisure industries in the '50s tend to ignore these contingent factors. Similar objections might be raised to the accusation that early Pop failed to "transcend . . . the ideology of affluence." The fixation of early Pop artists like Hamilton on consumer goods and synthetic materials (". . . the interplay of fleshy plastic and smooth, fleshier metal"[27] and his "search for what is epic in everyday objects and everyday attitudes"[28]) may now seem (dis)ingenuous and improbable, but seem less so when considered against the background of the real changes in consumption patterns which lay behind the rhetoric of the "new Golden Age." After all, the '50s did see a dramatic, unprecedented rise in living standards in Britain. No doubt the increases in spending power and rates of acquisition were not evenly distributed across all social classes, (the "invisible poor" remained invisible, deprivation persisted in relative terms) but the general improvement in material conditions was real enough.

As Christopher Booker puts it:

Between 1956 and the end of 1959 the country's hire purchase debt rose faster and by a greater amount overall, than at any other time before or since ... Deep Freeze had arrived and TV Instant Dinners and Fish Fingers and Fabulous pink Camay. And with so many bright new packages on the shelves, so many new gadgets to be bought, so much new magic in the dreary air of industrial Britain, there was a feeling of modernity and adventure that would never be won so easily again. For never again would so many English families be buying their first car, installing their first refrigerator, taking their first continental holiday. Never again could such ubiquitous novelty be found as in that dawn of the age of affluence.[29]

After the Depression and Austerity, for artists to refuse to respond positively to such transformations (overstated as they may be here by Booker), could seem more like sour grapes than a transcendence of prevailing ideology.

99

The third phase of Pop requires a different syle of invocation; less clearly focused on a precise time span, even less restricted to the work of individual artists as befits the moment of Pop's dispersal into the wider cultural streams ... a lightening up of tone for the salad days of Pop. I begin at the very end of the '60s.

In 1969, David Bailey and Peter Evans produced a book of photographs called *Goodbye Baby and Amen* as a kind of affectionate farewell to a scene, a moment, a social milieu which since 1965—thanks to *Time* magazine—had been described in the press as *Swinging London*. The book contains some 160 black and white Bailey portraits of what Peter Evans calls in his introduction,

the original cast of characters, the stars and near stars, the bit players, the winners and the terrible losers, the dead, who between them got the show on the King's Road.[30]

Amongst the faces of actors, stage and film directors, rock musicians, fashion designers, photographers and models, we find—and it's appropriate—Jim Dine, David Hockney, Peter Blake, Andy Warhol. The Pop artists are keywords in Bailey's litany, his hymn to "no deposit, non-returnable disposable fame,"[31] the theme which provides the book with a rationale and guaranteed sales of at least 160 copies. The artists' faces fit. In fact, the only face which looks out of place here belongs to Daniel Cohn-Bendit, Danny the Red, student activist and spokesman for the Continental student movement of '68.

Bailey does not try to hide the fact that Cohn-Bendit is only distantly related to the others. The print, of course, isn't meant to look as if it's taken from real life.

Just as Bardot in the book is blurred and soft-focus like a wet dream, like a film still, like a fan's poster to indicate her status as myth, as Sex Goddess, so the TV image epitomizes the distance which separates the world of current affairs—the real world where real things really happen—from the world of Swinging London. Danny the Red, refugee from the front pages, at sea amongst the center spreads and gossip column figures is presented here as second hand news, perhaps a little threatening, coming near the center of the book, a stone inside the candyfloss. It is a picture of a picture, an image at one remove. And our attention is drawn to the lines which mediate yet constitute the TV image for us as intentionally, as emphatically as in a Lichtenstein painting our attention is drawn to the Ben Day dots which compose the cartoon image.

In both pictures, that is what is drawn: our attention. In both cases, that is what is depicted: our status as spectators, our relation to the image. Our attention, in both instances, is directed to the mediations, to use a term from video, the "generations," degenerations which mark off the TV image or the comic stereotype from any referent in the real. The Bailey photograph and the Lichtenstein painting teach the same lesson: that the message is the material of which the message is composed is the medium in which it is transmitted. In other words, the McLuhanite tautology. The message in a Lichtenstein painting or a Warhol print or the Bailey photograph is that in this art, as in "mass art," to use Paul Barker's words, "the art lies on the surface."[32] "Its secret depth," to use his words again, "is that it has no secret depth."[33] In Warhol's words, "There's nothing behind it." James Brown, the black American soul singer, another '60s icon, like Warhol a master of banal repetition, makes the same point on a track entitled "E.S.P." where, against an insistent rhythmic backing, Brown repeats the phrase: "IT IS WHAT IT IS" again and again until voice and backing become indistinguishable and Brown can declaim on the nature of rhythm in rhythm . . . reminding us that that which is obvious matters, that the surfaces matter, that the surface is matter.

I quote James Brown here not just because he is an authentic spokesman for the popular arts, not just because like Lichtenstein, Barker, Bailey, Warhol he refuses to comply with the perennial art or music critic's request to talk "in depth," to explicate, to "get to the heart of the matter" (though he does indeed refuse to speak that other language). I quote him because if Pop Art teaches us nothing else, it teaches us the art of facetious quotation, of quotation out of context. After all, Pop Art was initially provocative precisely because it quoted "matter out of place."

[**Kitsch is**] . . . *vicarious experience and faked sensations . . . the epitome of all that is spurious in the life of our time.* (Clement Greenberg)

This brings us back, finally, to the objections leveled within art criticism against Pop. For those criticisms, like Greenberg's famous denunciation of kitsch, often revolve around Pop's ambivalence towards its raw material, its parasitic relation to the genuinely popular arts. Pop, it is frequently suggested, was indulgent and decadent because it refused to adopt a morally consistent and responsible line on the commercially structured popular culture which it invades, plunders and helps to perpetuate. Its ambiguity is culpable because Pop exploits its own contradictions instead of seeking to resolve them. It is morally reprehensible because it allows itself to be contained by the diminished possibilities that Capitalism makes available. Clearly, for British Pop artists in the late '60s, "Americanized" pictorial forms had come to stand—as Americanized science fiction had for post dadaist intellectuals in the '40s and '50s—as a hermeneutic: a cage full of codes and little else. But whereas, in former modernist appropriations of popular culture, the coded nature of these fictional worlds could serve (as it did in Boris Vian's thrillers or Godard's *Alphaville*) as an analogy for a constricted and alienated experience, in Pop Art and kitsch, the pull towards metaphor is arrested, the metaphors—where they exist at all—tend to be "Ostractions": jockey asides.[34] A vicarious and attenuated relation to authentic experience is taken for granted, even welcomed for the possibilities it opens up for play, disguise, conceit. To use Paolozzi's words, "The unreality of the image generated by entirely mechanical means *is commensurate with* the new reality with which we have lived for half a century but which has yet to make serious inroads on the established reality of art."[35]

Pop, then, refuses to deploy that potential for transcendence that Marcuse claimed characterizes the Great (European) Tradition. It refuses to abandon the ground of irony, to desert surface and style.

However, it is precisely here, on the reflective surfaces of Pop, that its potentially critical and iconoclastic force can be located. For the "politics" of Pop reside in the fact that it committed the cardinal sin in art by puncturing what Bourdieu calls the "high seriousness" upon which bourgeois art depends and through which it asserts its difference from the "debase" and "ephemeral" forms of "low" and "non"-art. (Even Dada had its "statements," its slogans . . .) Pop's "politics" reside in the fact that it was witty, decorative and had visible effects on the look of things, on the looking at things in the way it opened up the range of critical and creative responses to popular culture available to those who possess a modicum of cultural capital. Its politics reside in the fact that, in its minimal transformations of the object, it worked to reduce or to problematize the distance which Bourdieu defines as being necessary for the maintenance of the "pure aesthetic gaze," the remote gaze, the pose of contemplation on the object rather than absorption in the object: that pure gaze which unites all elitist taste formations:

. . . the theory of pure taste has its basis in a social relation: the antithesis between culture and corporeal pleasure (or nature if you will) and is rooted in the opposition between a cultivated bourgeoisie and the people.[36]

Pop did not break down that opposition, far from it, but it did manage to smudge the line more effectively than most other modern art movements. For whereas pure taste identifies itself in the active "refusal of the vulgar, the popular, and the purely sensual," Pop reaches out to close those gaps in order to produce not "politics" opposed to "pleasure" but rather something new: a politics of pleasure.

This is perhaps what guarantees Pop's continued exile from those places where the serious critical business of analyzing both Art and popular culture is conducted.

And yet an embryonic study of popular culture focusing on the conflict between popular aspirations and entrenched interests (taste makers) and proposing a model of cultural consumption which stresses class and regional differences was already being developed—albeit somewhat intuitively—by Alloway, Hamilton, McHale and the Smithsons during the mid to late '50s. For instance, as early as 1959, Alloway was arguing against the mass society thesis (which stilll haunted cultural studies "proper"—Hoggart et al):

We speak for convenience about a mass audience but it is a fiction. The audience today is numerically dense but highly diversified ... Fear of the Amorphous Audience is fed by the word "mass." In fact, audiences are specialized by age, sex, hobby, occupation, mobility, contacts, etc. Although the interests of different audiences may not be rankable in the curriculum of the traditional educationalist, they nevertheless reflect and influence the diversification which goes with increased industrialization.[37]

In the same article, Alloway quotes a reader's reaction to a science fiction magazine cover from the early '50s:

I'm sure Freud could have found much to comment and write on about it. Its symbolism, intentionally or not, is that of man, the victor; woman, the slave. Man the active, woman subjective; possessive man, submissive woman! ... What are the views of other readers on this? Especially in relation with Luros' backdrop of destroyed cities and vanquished man?[38]

Alloway merely quotes this in order to suggest that there are possibilities for a *private and personal deep interpretation* of the mass media beyond a purely sociological consideration of their functions. What is perhaps interesting for us (and so often repressed) is that a rudimentary home-grown semiotic—one poised to "demystify" "representations" of "gendered subjects" appears to be developing here in the correspondence columns of *Science Fiction Quarterly* in 1953 without any assistance from French academics (Barthes' *Mythologies* remained untranslated until 1972).

However, that hardly matters because the true legacy of Pop is not located in painting or purely academic analysis at all, but rather in graphics, fashion and popular music, in cultural and subcultural production.

For instance, the Sex Pistols' career, managed with a spectacular Warhol-like flair by Malcolm McLaren, another '60s Art School product, offered precisely the same kind of parodic, mock serious commentary on rock as a business that Pop Art in the '60s provided on the Art Game.

The principle of facetious quotation has been applied to subcultural fashion to produce what Vivienne Westwood used to call "confrontation dressing," collage dressing, genre dressing: the sartorial insignia of that elite which Peter York calls "Them" ...

Facetious quotation applied to music has produced the art of musical pastiche, word salad, aural cut ups, the art of sound quotation: the new musical genres, rap, dub, electronic and "constructed sound" ...

The final destination of Pop Art, Pop imagery and Pop

representational techniques lies not inside the gallery but rather in that return to the original material, that turning back towards the source which characterized so much of Pop Art's output in its classic phases. Its final destination lies, then, in the generation, regeneration not of Art with a capital A but of popular culture with a small "pc" . . .

Notes:

1) *Pop Art in England. Beginnings of a New Figuration 1947-63,* 1976, York City Gallery.

2) Richard Smith, *Ark 32,* Journal of the Royal College of Art, Summer 1962. In John Russell & Suzi Gablik, *Pop Art Redefined,* Thames & Hudson, 1969.

3) Jonathan Miller, *New Statesman,* May 1964.

4) Tom Wolfe, Bob and Spike in *The Pump House Gang,* Bantam, 1969.

5) Sidney Tillim, "Further Observations on the Pop Phenomenon" in *Artforum,* 1965. In Michael Compton, *Pop Art,* Hamlyn, 1970.

6) Mark Twain, *Innocents Abroad.*

7) Lawrence Alloway, "The Long Front of Culture," 1959, in *Cambridge Opinion,* Cambridge University, 1959, reprinted in Russell & Gablik, op. cit., 1969. This phrase occurs in a comparison between Hitchcock's films before and after the War. It is presented as an allegory for a more general shift in cultural values from the pre-War fixation on manly action to the '50s absorption in image:
In the pre-War Thirty Nine Steps, *the hero wore tweeds and got a little rumpled as the chase wore on, like a gentleman farmer after a day's shooting. In* North by North West *(1959), the hero is an advertising man . . . and though he is hunted from New York to South Dakota, his clothes stay neatly Brooks Brothers. That is to say, the dirt, sweat and damage of pursuit are less important than the package in which the hero comes —the tweedy British gentleman or the urbane Madison Avenue man . . . The point is that the drama of possessions (in this case, clothes) characterizes the hero as much as (or more than) his motivations and actions . . .*

8) Ivan Karp, "Anti-Sensibility Painting," in *Artforum,* 1963, reprinted in Compton, op. cit., 1970.

9) See Paul Barker, "Art nouveau riche" in Paul Barker, (ed), *Arts in Society*, Fontana, 1977.

10) John McHale, "The Fine Arts and the Mass Media," in *Cambridge Opinion*, 1959, reprinted in Russell and Gablik, op. cit., 1969.

11) Reyner Banham, "Representations in Protest," in Barker (ed), op. cit., 1977.

12) Robert Indiana, "What is Pop Art? Interview with eight painters," Gene Swanson, "What is Pop Art? Interviews with eight painters," *Art News*, Nov. 1963, reprinted in Russell & Gablik, op. cit., 1969. The quote is taken from an interview with Indiana. The next sentence is worth quoting too:
[*Pop*] *is basically a U-turn back to representational visual communication, moving at a breakaway speed in several sharp late models ... some young painters turn back to some less exalted things like Coca Cola, ice cream sodas, big hamburgers, supermarkets and EAT signs. They are eye hungry, they pop ... [They are] not intellectual, social and artistic malcontents with furrowed brows and fur-lined skulls ...*

13) Uwe M. Schneede, *Paolozzi*, Thames & Hudson, 1971.

14) Lawrence Alloway, op. cit., 1959.

15) John Canaday, "Pop Art sells on and on. Why," in *The New York Times*, 1964, reprinted in Compton, op. cit., 1970.

16) Irving Sandler, review of New Realists exhibition (in the *New York Post*, 1962, reprinted in Compton, op. cit., 1970. The full quote is illuminating:
The coming together of fine and commercial art must have contributed to the wide recognition that New Realism has received. No other manifestation in recent years has been given as much attention so quickly in the slick magazines. Ad men (and others who share their approach) have probably promoted New Realism because it flatters their own 'art'. And they have also been able to apply it to their own work.

17) Peter Fuller, "The Crisis in British Art," in *Artforum*, 1977.

18) Hugh Adams, *Art of the Sixties*, Phaidon, 1978.

19) Lynda Morris, "What made the Sixties' Art so Successful, so Shallow" in *Art Monthly*, 1976.

20) *Paolozzi*, op. cit.

21) Dick Hebdige, "Towards a Cartography of Taste, 1935-62," in *Block* 3, 1981.

22) John Blake, "Space for Decoration," in *Design* 77, 1959.

23) Richard Hoggart, *The Uses of Literacy*, Penguin, 1958.

24) Ibid.

25) Lawrence Alloway, op. cit., 1959.

26) Richard Hoggart, op. cit., 1958. Of course, there was still an adherence to fine art

values even amongst the original proponents of Pop. In order to underline the fact that transformational work had indeed been performed upon the original subject-matter, Hamilton (in marked contrast to Warhol) tended to stress just how elaborate the process of "cooking" had become, no matter how plain and simple the original ingredients:

One work began as an assemblage assisted with paint, was then photographed, the photograph modified and a final print made which was itself added to paint and collage. Quoted in Compton, op. cit., 1970

27) Richard Hamilton, quoted in *Pop Art in England*, 1976.

28) Richard Hamilton, "An Exposition of $ he," in *Architectural Design*, October, 1962.

29) Christopher Booker, *The Neophiliacs*, Collins, 1969.

30) David Bailey & Peter Evans, *Goodbye Baby and Amen*, Corgi, 1972.

31) Ibid.

32) Paul Barker, introduction to Barker (ed.), op. cit., 1977.

33) Ibid.

34) Gerard Cordesse, "The Impact of American Science Fiction," in *Europe in Super-culture: American Popular Culture and Europe*, (ed) C.W.E. Bigsby, Paul Elek Press, 1975.

35) *Paolozzi* op. cit.

36) Pierre Bourdieu, "The Aristocracy of Culture," in *Media Culture and Society*, Vol 2, no 3, 1980.

37) Lawrence Alloway, op. cit., 1959.

38) *Science Fiction Quarterly*, reader quoted, Ibid.

PUNK: POLITICAL POP
DAN GRAHAM

Note:
All the material this article makes reference to what happened in 1976 and 1977. Punk is now past history.

USA Punk I

The Ramones from New York City and Devo from Akron, Ohio model their aesthetic/political strategies after those Pop artists in the 1960s who preferred to package themselves rather than be packaged by the media or the record industry. Devo suggests that this is in order for them not to be tricked by the media/corporate structure of "the business":

We figured we'd mimic the structure of those who get the greatest rewards out of the upside-down business and become a corporation ... Why stop at the music? I really believe that's a mistake groups make. They don't understand the total picture that they fit into. They don't see how they interrelate publicly to the culture and the political situation in their work. They are destroyed because they

111

become exploited by the system. Like, take a group, divide them up,
pull one person out as the star and make solo albums ... We decided
that what we hated about rock and roll was STARS ... we watched
Roxy Music, a band we liked, slowly become Bryan Ferry and Roxy
Music. If you get a band that's good, you bust it up and sell 3 times as
many records. Take the Beatles for example.

They broaden this critique of 1960s rock and roll to a
critique of United States corporate capitalism, recognizing the
covert function of rock in consumer society as propaganda for
its myths of individualism.

What do you think rock and roll is in America ... besides Propa-
ganda for Corporate Capitalist Life? Most rock musicians; they're no
more than clerks or auto mechanics, you know ... if they're lucky
they'll settle into an Alice Cooper kind of existence ... Since pop
music is definitely a vulgar art form connected with consumerism,
the position of any artist is, in pop entertainment, really self-
contempt. Hate what you like, like what you hate. It's a totally
schizophrenic position, but that in itself is a principle that most
people both in the business and outside it don't understand. There-
fore, if they don't understand that very idea, they don't even know
what they're dealing with. Devo understands its self-contradiction
and uses it as the basis for its creativity ... The system is totally
geared toward profit, obviously. The artist is usually a willing victim
because he's middle-class shit himself.

Devo sees its conceptual role in tearing down the myths
and assumptions of the 1960s: "All that everybody still thinks
is hip or beautiful." They aim to "remake and remodel" their

sources in order to create a new, synthetic or reconstituted form, analogous to DNA or biological hybrids. By this means they can parallel/parody/put into perspective the process by which corporations synthesize new consumable products:

It's taking genetic structures and mutating them, comparing them with other structures . . . like putting a monkey's head on a human baby . . . reordering things and seeing the same things differently . . . What we did is we . . . just took everything that was happening, cut it apart, and restructured it from a 180 degree angle from where it had been. Merely taking everything that is not emphasized and emphasizing it in order to create reflection. Jumbling up everyone's assumptions, everyone's vested interests, everyone's smug viewpoint.

Their remakes of the Rolling Stones' "Satisfaction" and "Sloppy (I Saw My Baby Gettin')" are examples of remodelling their sources. To begin with, the latter's title has been altered, putting "Sloppy" before, rather than after, "I Saw My Baby Gettin'." Both songs work by deconstructing and then robotically rebuilding music and lyrical phrasing. The macho assumptions of the songs (which tend to link male aggression and assertive sexuality to man's connections with primitive animals) are androgenized by the use of an electronic-synthesizer that disembodies the sound. These hybrids are welded together by a "football, half-time drum beat . . . like cheerleaders and marching bands at a football game" in order to instigate group "sing-along" feelings. This effectively breaks down the song's original underlying assumptions: myths of free sexuality and individualism. The message of the typical

'60s song, addressed to the self-identity of the listener, served to condition him/her, just as advertisements in the media condition him/her for a role as a consumer of lifestyles. Devo sees rock and roll as quasi-disciplinary exercise conditioning the typical American consumer to buy more from big corporations. They are in agreement with the *lyrics* of "Satisfaction," but see the song's stylistic/performance assumptions as supporting the individualist mythology and corporate-induced consumerism which the song's lyrics allegedly undermine:

When I'm watchin' my TV / And that man comes on to tell me / How white my shirts can be / Well he can't be a man 'cause he doesn't smoke / The same cigarettes as me / I can't get no satisfaction / I can't get me no satisfaction . . .
From *Satisfaction* (Jagger and Richards)

When Devo orchestrates the Stones' numbers to a disco-like beat which owes something to Donna Summer and something to Kraftwerk, they are deliberately playing on the assumption that punks are against disco and are thus anti-lower-class black/Italian/Hispanic music. The corporate rock industry prefers to divide minority groups into separate markets. This division sets up an ideological opposition between groups: one which works in favor of the dominant ideology when it pits one minority ideology against another. Here Devo upsets punk assumptions by its use of disco, and upsets disco assumptions by its use of punk corrosiveness. While media representations place the attitudes and trends in isolated opposition, Devo prefers to broaden its potential audience and to place both attitudes in tension/perspective. If a song is both disco and punk at the same time, it can be read in both ways; it is equally a parody of both viewpoints. Equivocal readings allow the songs to put into perspective, and corrode the underlying assumptions of both constituent audiences. It also enables Devo to locate what punk and disco have in common: the elimination of the spectator's passivity in favor of a "do-it-yourself" attitude in the production of spectacle. Disco and punk both share a quasi-military beat that forces the audience into a collective engagement with the music on the level of its own production. Punk and disco dancing as mass phenomena resemble the propaganda spectacles of the 1930s, clearly opposed to the "do-your-own-thing," introspective "hippie" and "post-hippieism" of the late 1960s and early 1970s, where the individual is the ultimate self-contained reference point.

UK Punk I

The English Punk movement, in contrast to the American, is suspicious of rock music as an art form, and of content other than direct, socially realistic propaganda. English punk is a phenomenon of the class system. As the dominant form of representation is an expression of the interests of the ruling class, it is difficult for a minority group to express disagreement with its values and to fairly represent its position in terms of art without its message (and form of expression) being censured, rejected, or questioned. This was made quite apparent to English punk rockers when the Sex Pistols' "God Save the Queen" (originally titled "No Future" and released in

115

the summer of 1977 on the occasion of Queen Elizabeth II's "Silver Jubilee") was quickly banned from British radio airplay. It was dropped from production by the Pistols' record company, which was then forced through media intimidation to drop the Sex Pistols as artists. Claiming that the Queen was a "figurehead . . . she ain't no human being," went too far in exposing the British myth in that year of England's extreme trade deficit. The myth of Elizabeth's "Jubilee Year" had the double function of attracting tourist money and proclaiming that there was a future for England, though this future depended upon preserving *status quo* assumptions. Controversy began when newspaper scare headlines proclaimed (inaccurately) that the song called the Queen "a moron." In fact, the song says that "the fascist regime . . . made you a moron," implying that the cult of personalizing the Queen is an Establishment decoy: that is, the Queen has no power in reality, so her "humanness" is beside the point—a duplicitous diversion.

God save the Queen / The fascist regime / It made you a moron / A potential H-bomb. / God save the Queen / She ain't no human being / There is no future / And England's dreaming. / No future / No future / No future for you. / God save the Queen. / We mean it man / We love our Queen / God says: / God save the Queen / Tourists are money / And our figurehead is not what she seems. / God save history / Save save your mad parade / Lord God have mercy / All crimes are paid / Where there's no future / How can there be sin? / We're the flowers in the dustbin / We're the poison in your human machine / We're the future / God save the Queen. From *God Save the Queen* (Sex Pistols).

Bourgeois cultural forms function to mediate relations between the dominant and the lower classes. The predominant form of cultural representation in a capitalist democracy is, like its form of government, a representational form: a fictional, self-contained "world" that stands for reality. Propagandistic artwork is, by contrast, an attack on the more liberal, realist art work. Representational work functions as does representational government; various points of view are depicted and mediated in place of direct conflict between the classes or forces which these mediated expressions correspond to in actual society. The subject or spectator is then free to pick and choose between points of view. He/she identifies with either point of view by identifying with one character or another, but is distanced from both the fictional world and actual engagement/conflict. Some examples, outside of the pop song, are the novel, fictional films, TV news stories, etc. ... in other words, any narrative form that places various characters in conflict. Propaganda, in opposition to this form, aligns the spectator in relation to depicted forces that exist outside and beyond the art work. Representational realism usually deals with a past situation, whereas propagandistic texts use current situations as subject matter. The classical realist text is closed; the conflict exists only within its fictional "space." In a narrative work, there is pressure to resolve the contradictions and conflicts through the conclusion. The propagandist text puts the spectator in contact with, in relation to, social practices existing outside the actual art work. The propagandist text speaks directly to the audience, addressing it as "you" or "we." It does not pretend to be disinterested or directed only toward a higher, artistic neutrality as does classical "high" art.

It also does not hide the ego of the spectator. As its subject matter is based on its function, it is ephemeral and not "timeless."

The Desperate Bicycles are typical of many amateur, self-recorded and produced English groups using the medium purely as propaganda.

One side of their second self-recorded single describes how they made their first self-recorded single for only 125 pounds and suggests that instead of being passive consumer-spectators, listeners go out and produce *their own* records. The second side picks up this refrain from the other side and extends it in essay-like argument, suggesting that listeners refrain from backing the neo-Nazi political party, the National Front. It also criticizes, from within, certain self-deceptions of the punk movement:

No time for spectating / Tune in, count it / Let it blast / Cut it, press it / Distribute it / Xerox music's here at last. / All you phoney Fascists / DON'T Back The Front! / You who trade on racist hate / Better learn some dialectic / Before it gets too late . . .
From *Don't Back The Front* (Desperate Bicycles)

The song's lyrics are momentary and urgent. They may be paraphrased as follows: 1) an appeal to prevent the media use/defuse/discredit the New Wave music scene by fashionably associating it with violence. 2) the audience listening to this record is urged/instructed to make their own records. They are addressed (and constituted by this from of address) as a group considered apart from a general mass audience. Passive record consumption is a trap. Listening to this record is seen as only a *preliminary* stage for the New Wave audience; the consumer should be led to the production of his own records and further meaning. 3) "We," in this specially activated group, are told that "it's (monopolistic) Capital," and not racial minorities (Asians or blacks) that takes "our" jobs away. For this reason "we" are advised not to give practical support or encouragement to the National Front, the party that blames unemployment on minority groups in Britain. This allies us with the viewpoint of "Rock Against Racism," a collective of New Wave musicians and leftists organized to encourage young, unemployed, working class whites not to vote for the National Front candidates, and to counter the misunderstanding caused by the media's equation of punk music with fascistic violence and anarchy.

Punk has had to deal with negative reactions to its assault upon liberal assumptions. By expressing disgust for and satirically deflating liberal society's repression of (its own) violence, punk itself came to be associated with the violence it was desublimating. The media took punk's satire of social violence literally because it wasn't neutralized or distanced by conventional representation: "The media have always tried to associate punk with violence. But like the Pistols—their violence is just a parody of violence and the papers took it literally." (Poly Styrine)

The notion of the "rock star," to paraphrase Devo, was part of the 1960s corporate marketing strategy. From the perspective of English Punk, this had certain class assumptions as well. Punks were aware: 1) that the '60s "superstar" was an artificial media myth, 2) that this myth and the "superstar's" position were tenuous, 3) that the "super-star" artist failed to perceive his position realistically. "Try to evade reality/And you're just a novelty" (Killjoys).

In the '60s, the Beatles had been (symbolically and economically) allowed to rise above their lower class origins, and to express oral (communal) values. Their rise was accomplished through "normal" opportunities: an art school education and utilization of a market system where rock music had become an important product. As they made money for themselves and also for the British economy, they achieved not only star status, but upper-middle class respectability. In fact, with their official recognition by the Queen, the Beatles ascended to pseudo-aristocracy. The mythological ascension of the Beatles was proof for Britain that the system worked; that the class system wasn't as repressive as some critics contended. It also proved that "art" and the attitudes fostered in English art school could produce "higher" values enabling a working class lad to rise above his common station and the grim reality of his childhood background. By contrast, punk was defiantly anti-art, and true to its class origins. Its lyrics offered no escape, "fun," or art-like transcendence of reality. Punk preferred using the local dialect, rather than affecting an American cultural accent. It preferred honest amateurism to (corporate) professionalism. It preferred sincere disgust and confusion. It asked questions, rather than sought stylistic spiritual solutions, which were alien to its own social realities or contradictions:

I don't want to know what the rich are doing / I don't want to go where the rich are going / They think they're so clever, they think they're so right / But the truth is only known by guttersnipes . . . /

We're a garageband and we come from garageland."
From *Garageland* by the Clash (Stummer and Jones).

What we're doing is similar to the hippies in the way that we're sort of protesting against certain things. But the way they done it was different—nonviolent: peace and love and all that stuff. Whereas it's not peace and love now: it's sort of hate and war . . . We're not saying, "Flowers, man." We're sort of pointing out the situation as it really is. I thought that the whole hippie thing was like evading reality—all that sort of stuff. It's quite different now. We're the revenge of the hippies. (Paul Simmon of the Clash)

On October 8, 1976, negotiating with a number of record companies, the Sex Pistols signed with EMI, the largest entertainment conglomerate in England. On November 26, 1976 their first single, *Anarchy in the UK* was released:

I am the anti-christ / I am an anarchist / I don't know what I want / But I know how to get it / I wanna destroy the passer-by / Cos I / I wanna be anarchy—no dog's body . . .

On December 1, 1976 the group appeared on Bill Grundy's Thames TV program, *Today:*

Grundy: *I'm told that the group received 40,000 pounds from a record company. Doesn't that seem . . . er . . . to be slightly opposed to their* (deep breath) *anti-materialistic view of life?*
Sex Pistols: No, the more the merrier.
BG: *Really?*
SP: We fuckin' spent it, ain't we?

121

BG: *Are you serious or are you just making me, trying to make me laugh?*

SP: No, it's gone. Gone.

BG: *Are you serious?*

SP: Mmm.

BG: *Beethoven, Mozart, Bach and Brahms have all died . . .*

SP: They're heroes of ours, ain't they . . . They really turn us on. Well, they're very . . .

BG: *Well, I suppose they turn other people on?*

SP: *(Mumbled).* That's their tough shit . . .

FAN: I've always wanted to meet you.

BG: *Did you really?*

SP: Yeah.

BG: (To a young woman accompanying the band) *We'll meet afterwards, shall we?* (Laughter).

SP: You dirty sod. You dirty old man.

BG: *We'll keep going chief, keep going.* (Pause). *Go on. You've got another five seconds. Say something outrageous.*

SP: You dirty bastard.

BG: *Go on, again.*

SP: You dirty fucker.

BG: *What a clever boy.*

SP: What a fucking rotter *(More laughter).*

BG: (Turning to face camera) *Well that's it for tonight. The other rocker, Eamonn, I'm not saying nothing about him, will be back tomorrow. I'll be seeing you soon. I hope I'm not seeing you* (to the band) *again. From me, though, goodnight.*

As a result of the interview the Pistols were banned throughout Britain from appearing live on stage and Thames TV suspended Bill Grundy. It was revealed that Thames was owned by the EMI conglomerate and great pressure was then placed on the company to fire the Sex Pistols. Leslie Hill of EMI recalls:

The people in EMI and also outside of EMI had different kinds of objections. Some objected to the four-letter words on television; some objected to the supposedly violent aspects of the whole thing; some objected to the word "anti-christ" in the song ... we couldn't promote the records in that situation. Supposing, for example, they were doing a tour. Now supposing we'd done what we usually do with them on tour, which is to have a press party or a party at the end of the tour. ... You imagine what would have happened. There would have been a riot ... You know, we've got hundreds of groups and hundreds of things to do. It gets to a point where it really isn't worth the trouble ... I said to them you go to a smaller ... label.

On March 9, 1977 the Sex Pistols signed with A & M Records. Seven days after the signing, after a raucous and widely press-covered party at A & M's corporate headquarters that received extremely alarming publicity, A & M terminated the Sex Pistols' contract at a total profit for the Pistols of 50,000 pounds. On their third try, they were definitely signed by Virgin Records.

It's an unlimited supply / And there is no reason why / I tell you, it was a frame / They only did it cause of fame / Who? / EMI-EMI-EMI ... And you thought that we were faking / That we were always money-making / You do not believe that we're for real / Or you would lose your cheap appeal / Don't you judge a book just by the cover / Unless you cover just another / And blind acceptance is a sign / Of stupid fools who stand in line / Like: / EMI-EMI-EMI ...
From *EMI* (Sex Pistols)

Perhaps it was manager Malcolm McLaren and the Sex Pistols' premeditated plan to focus the inherent destructiveness symbolized by rock onto rock's real relation to the media; they used to it promote the group. To use the media to become famous in order to destroy the media and media-created fame; in other words, to show it for what it was by forcing the media system's contradictions (and their contradictions as a rock act) into the open was the Pistols' ultimate goal. When the Sex Pistols arrived in New York for their U.S. tour, reporters demanded to take photos of Johnny Rotten. He refused unless he was paid $5.00 per photo. They naturally assumed that all rock stars wanted publicity, any kind, and that he would relinquish control of his public image, and allow himself to be freely manipulated by the press. The story was reported in the press, without photos. In the Sex Pistols' song, "I Wanna Be Me" (the flip side of *Anarchy in the UK*), this aspect of Rotten's relationship to his public media image is depicted in terms of a psychological identity crisis, both for media-makers and spectators, as well as for performers. The spectator, positioned so she/he is looking for an identity, via the stars, "turns the pages and stare(s) at the magazine . . . turns to the stars . . . to be brainwash(ed)." The rock star sees that both spectator and media-maker "wanna be me . . . wanna be someone through someone."

Turn the page and stare at the magazine / I want to be on telly or— / This is brainwash and this is a clue / Turn to the stars, who fool you / Tell me why, you can't explain / You're only looking for— / Didn't they fool you / They want to be you. / If we were free, we could live again / You didn't fool me / I fooled you. / You wanna be

/ Yeah wanna be me / You wanna be someone through someone /
Yeah, didn't I fool you / I ruined you / You, didn't I fool you / I
sussed you out.
From *You Wanna Be Me* (Sex Pistols)

Many British punk songs attack television as an institution, for as The Clash put it in *London's Burning:* "Everybody's drowning in a sea of television." Their "I'm So Bored With The USA" sees television as a conditioner of working-class acquiescence through its escapist mythology and, more menacingly, as a vehicle for American cultural domination:

Yankee soldier, he wanted to attack / The men in Cambodia / But
now he's fallen back. / Yankee automation / He's the dictator of the
world. / And they can't afford to miss a word. / I'm so bored with
the USA / I'm so bored with the USA / But what can I do. / Yankee
detectives are always on the TV / Cause killers in America / Work
seven days a week / Never mind the Stars and Stripes / Let's read
the Watergate Tapes. / . . . etc.
From *I'm So Bored With The USA* (Strummer and Jones)

The group Alternative TV evolved from the editorial staff of the first punk news-magazine, *Sniffing Glue.* In their performances they attempt to question the notion of "giving the audience what it wants." They encourage it to use the band as a framework for collective political expression/questioning. Their live set features a "soap-box" section, where members of the audience can come on stage and speak their minds. Their intention is to break down the usually passive, powerless position in which spectators are placed in their relation to the musical spectacle (to their performing "heroes" on stage). Part of the ideal of English punk rock is that no one, not even groups, is to dictate ideas or behavior-norms for anyone else— to be an ego-ideal. (The exhibitionism of the previous star system had encouraged rock performers to live their lives as fantasy surrogates for their voyeuristic followers.) *The Image Has Cracked,* the first album by ATV has an extract from a less than successful soap-box session, in which Mark Perry of the group chastises those who have spoken but have had nothing to say. Intercut with this session is a recording taken from a conventional television program of a spokesman extolling The Other Cinema. (The Other Cinema was an alternative cinema-house which, in addition to new films, featured open political discussions on Sunday nights by New Wave musicians, writers and audience members.)

Mark Perry: *This is the period in the show where we ask members of the audience to come up on stage and say what they would about particular subjects. Anybody who wants to come up, come up now . . . There must be one of you who wishes to use this particular soap-box we've been standing on . . . You can have three minutes.*
First Person: *You're thick, right?* (**Audience:** *No!*), *What do you mean, "No?" Some of you know nothing . . . O.K. mate, seeing as though you know nothing, all right, all right . . . How many of you are over 18? . . . Now a lot of you people have been influenced by the Prime Minister, right?* (**Audience:** *No!*), *You fucking listen, fucking listen to me, right.* (**First Voice:** *Shut up!* **Second Voice:** *Let him speak!*) *Right. What's your fucking favorite TV programs, then?* (**Audience:** *babble of different replies*) *See, all you people watch fucking "Coronation Street." It's your favorite TV program,*

126

right? . . . If you really took action . . . see the people running the country . . . If you took action right . . .

Mark Perry: *We do not want bouncers on the stage. We are spoilsports. The only people we want on the stage are those who want to say something. Will the bouncers please get off . . .*

Second Person: *My name is Ivan Johnson. One of our group was killed two weeks ago. We are looking for a singer. Anybody who wishes to audition, just leave your name at the desk. May the dead rise. You want to go? Well fucking leave your name . . .*

Mark Perry: *Right. You stupid bastards get off the stage. Right. One of you people gets a chance to say something and what happens, there's a fight. It's not very cool. That's something you can do is fight. I just wanted to make a point. I love all you people, but I hate you when you act like stupid idiots. Because that's how they grind you down.*

(Cut to TV Program)

Spokesman: *In this space, films have been seen by over 8,000 people in its first year of existence. Films, that but for this cinema, would well have remained in their cans. Here also battles are fought, imaginations expressed, differences confronted—and it also is space where all kinds of movements can develop . . .*

(Cut back to soap-box session)

Mark Perry: *Even rock and roll. A lot of people think it good that when the Buzzcocks and Sex Pistols and the Tridents and all that lot, I love those bands and I'm not putting 'em down, everybody thinks it's great that they are on TV, but it's not, is it? Because what you're getting is diluted, diluted shit. Everybody is so pleased, oh fine, we've got punk on TV. Oh, we've won. No way have you won . . . Someone said, "We know the problem, what is the answer?" This is really depressing, because I have no fucking answer.*

USA Punk II

In contrast to the seriousness of the English groups, the Ramones (and in general the American New Wave) utilize a satiric, Pop Art-like ironic distance and a musical (rock and roll) neo-classicism in manipulating their image, relative to media images. Like Andy Warhol or Roy Lichtenstein, they package themselves, as well as their music, based on media stereotypes. They stay in advance of the media or industry packaging them because they are a product of their own packaging. Like American Pop Art, the Ramones' lyrics use pre-packaged mass cultural clichés, but their use of these images is ironically humorous. The sincere, confessional "I" of such songwriters-performers as Jackson Browne, Neil Young or Van Morrison is rejected, as is their introspection and romanticism. The Ramones' attitude toward their songs is not unlike that stated by Lichtenstein in 1963:

Art . . . has become extremely romantic and unrealistic . . . it is utopian. It has had less to do with the world, it looks inward . . . neo-Zen and all that. This is not so much a criticism as an obvious observation. Outside is the world; it's there. Pop Art looks out into the world; it appears to accept its environment, which is not good or bad but different—another state of mind.

Beat on the brat / Beat on the brat / Beat on the brat with a baseball bat / Oh yeah, oh yeah, uh-oh / What can you do? / What can you do? / With a brat like that always on your back / What can you do? (lose?)
From *Beat on the Brat* (The Ramones)

In the beginning that anti-intellectual pose was juss a pose. And it was an intellectual pose in itself, 'cos everyone was fed up with bein' intellectual. But they are all really clever people, they juss got into that for a laugh. It's juss like anti-art . . . There were a lot of serious things to punk, yet it's totally ludicrous.
—Poly Styrine

PT-boat on the way to Havana / I used to make a living, man / Pickin' the banana / Now I'm a guide for the CIA / Hooray for the USA! / Baby, baby make me loco / Baby, baby, make me mambo. / Sent to spy on a Cuban talent show / First stop—Havana au go-go / Pickin' the banana / Hoorah for Havana!
From *Havana Affair* (The Ramones)

The heroes depicted in comic books are fascist types, but I don't take them seriously in these paintings—maybe there is a point in not taking them seriously, a political point.
—Roy Lichtenstein

Lichtenstein is ambivalent about whether he wants to consider his work "political." In American culture, to define a work as ostensively political automatically categorizes it as academic or high art; mass culture will have little interest in it, because it assumes a patronizing attitude. As a category, "the political" is negatively coded; it means "no fun." The Ramones are fun.

Like Lichtenstein's images, the Ramones' songs are comic strip stereotypes of American pop culture, the post-Vietnam violence repressed by mainstream American pop music's mellowed-out, laid-back, higher consciousness, "Made in L.A." sound. Placed back in the popular culture, their songs become capable of dual (and ironic) readings; the popular or vernacular reading and a second reading which puts into perspective or quotes the first reading. Like Lichtenstein, the Ramones classicize their immediate sources, relating them to earlier rock and roll (earlier stereotyped popular culture) lyrics and musical conventions. Their first album, *The Ramones,* was constructed from basic 1950s musical forms and references. Their second album, *Leave Home,* with its remake of "California Sun," and more definitively, the next album, *Rocket to Russia,* adopt a 1960s Californian "surfing sound" with its established connotations of "fun." Ironically, they choose to apply the "fun" idea to New York City (thought by the rest of the country to be the opposite of a "fun" spot) in "Rockaway Beach," and to punk as a media image in "Sheena is a Punk Rocker" and "Ramona." The Ramones' neo-classicism is very 1970s. (The real social confusion of the present is masked by a neatly packaged recreation of just-past halcyon time.) Recent history up to ten years ago is broken into a confusion of delimited self-contained decades; first the '30s, then the '50s, and now the '60s are being revived. The public's access to these magic eras is further confused with personal nostalgia: history as memory: memory associated by the media with the time "when we grew up." In media representations the present appears to be confused with the particular past being revived. The Ramones present the musical forms of this revival, but eliminate the nostalgically personalized (social) content. In films and in TV series such as "Happy Days," "The Waltons," and "Laverne and Shirley," one sees the projection of present-day, largely middle-class problems, represented by lower-middle class characters (possibly our family forebears, one generation back) situated in the half-accurately/half-nostalgically depicted decade of the '50s, the '30s, '40s, or the '60s. The Ramones give us lower-middle class images of the 1970s (albeit it from a comic strip):

... We're a happy family / Me mom and daddy / Sitting here in Queens / Eating refried beans / We're in all the magazines / Gulpin' down thorazines. / We ain't got no friends / Our troubles never end / No Christmas cards to send / Daddy likes men / Daddy's telling lies / Baby's eating flies / Mommy's on pills / Baby's got the chills. / I'm friends with the president / I'm friends with the pope / We're all making a fortune / Selling daddy's dope.
From *We're A Happy Family* (The Ramones)

UK Punk II

The problem for punk is how to present its critique of the corporate system in the form of a product that is, by definition, part of the system. It must also discover how to represent its political stance from inside media representations controlled by liberals. Tom Robinson, lead singer and main song-writer of the Tom Robinson Band, is both a Marxist and a gay activist. TRB has been heavily promoted and packaged by EMI, the company that dropped the Pistols, perhaps because TRB's commitment to a specific cause is acceptable from a liberal viewpoint; because the group would have a definite market appeal to gays as a large minority group. Rather than be defined by the media as anarchist or punk, Tom Robinson wishes to use his leverage with EMI to further his and the band's extra-musical political purposes. For example, printed on the back of their record's cover is the statement:

Politics isn't party broadcasts and general elections, it's your kid sister who can't get an abortion, your best mate getting paki-bashed, or sent down for processing one joint of marijuana ... it's everyday life for rock fans, for everyone who hasn't got a cushy job or rich parents. I got no illusions about the political left anymore than the right; just a shrewd idea which of the two sides' gonna stomp on us first. All of us—you, me, rock and rollers, punks, jobless, dope smokers, squatters, unmarried mothers, gays, the jobless immigrants, gipsies ... And if we fail, if we get swallowed up by big business before we achieve a thing, then we'll havta face the scorn of tomorrow's generation. But we're gonna have a good try. Fancy joining us?
—Tom Robinson on *New Music Express*

On the back cover there are appeals to join specific political organizations, giving addresses to write for further information.

Tom explains how he presents their song "Sing if You're Glad to Be Gay" to the general audience: "If you walk straight on and sing *Sing If You're Glad to Be Gay*, you get all sorts of limp-wrist gestures and take-the-piss-out-of-fags business ... The words 'gaylib' are enough to bring a snicker to every locker room. People don't respond rationally to the subject. Women sense rivalry in it and men sense a threat to their masculinity. At small gigs where we played most of our working life, these self-same macho drunks, the rowdy element in every audience, are the ones that are gonna cause trouble." They usually begin the set with "Martin," a song about male bonding, "delivered in the person of a working-class hoodlum swilling a bit of beer meself, talking about beating up kids at school, getting nicked by the police . . . They think it's great, raising their beer glasses and cheering. They're in there with you. Then you start *Glad to Be Gay* with 'The British police are the best in the world' . . . and they say, 'Yeah, right, mate! Bloody right! I've been drunk and disorderly on a Saturday night!' And then you hit them with the chorus, and by then they're already involved. And that way you don't get beaten up as you walk out the stage door."

The British police are the best in the world / I don't believe one of those stories I've heard / About them raiding our pubs for no reason at all / Lining up customers by the wall / Pickin' out people, knocking them down / Resisting arrest as they're kicked on the ground / Searching their houses / Calling them queer / I don't believe that sort of thing happens here. / Sing if you're glad to be gay / Sing if you're happy to be that way / Hey, sing if you're glad to be gay / Sing if you're happy that way.

If punk is purely propagandistic, the system's response is to censure it, as liberal media-consciousness sees propaganda (left or right) as totalitarianism. Instead, the liberal position affirms the right for all classes and opinions to be equally represented. Any "truth" presented in a subjective or emotional fashion would, in the liberal system's view, bias or distort the receiver's openness to alternative views. Liberal media wishes to view (represent) the world "objectively," where various opinions are evenly balanced and framed.

Because statements can be represented (distanced/objectified) by being put into perspective, they need not be experienced/confronted by the spectator. Although it would like to appear to be objective, the liberal view is a product of middle-class interests/consciousness. Art and political representation are linked by a mediated "perspective." In the same way that free trade economics produces the political notion of free expression of various viewpoints, this philosophy is transformed, in art, into the notion of the free expression of the individual artist's viewpoint.

White Riot / Black men have a lot of problems / But they don't mind throwing a brick / But white men have got too much school / Where they teach you to be thick / So we're content, we don't resent / We go reading papers and wearing slippers / White riot! White riot! / I wanna riot / White riot! A riot of my own.
From *White Riot* by the Clash (Strummer and Jones)

"White Riot" was written after troubles broke out at the annual Notting Hill Carnival (organized by the area's black immigrants). Although newspaper reports implied it was the blacks who rioted against the police who were protecting innocent tourists, the events were more complex. In addition to merrymaking, the event had become an occasion for various leftist groups to propagandize to both black and white celebrants. That year the right-wing National Front counter-demonstrated against the leftists at the Carnival and was attacked by both leftists and blacks. The police interceded to separate the two groups, but seemed to do this in the Front's favor and to bully black people. Some blacks counter-attacked and a police riot ensued. In a sense the police represented (to the blacks) all the under-the-surface hatred and anger that lower-middle class whites have harbored against Jamaican immigrants for years. Two years of successive and serious riots helped make evident that beneath the facade of the "Silver Jubilee," Britain was having difficulty accepting its new position as a poor and multi-racial society. Among its working-class, the Pakistani and Jamaican Commonwealth arrivals were rising toward the middle-class faster than native whites. "White Riot" is partly an answer to white hate directed toward the blacks. But, unlike the upper-middle class liberal attitude, it doesn't attempt to sentimentalize the "black problem" away or to appeal to the concept of a universal brotherhood that doesn't exist. Young white singers appropriated black music and slanted it towards a white, teenage audience (and market). Black music (representing black ideology) and white music (representing white ideology) are never precisely compatible. In dealing with blacks, white music either sentimentalizes the black's plight or seeks a transcendental synthesis of both realities. A classical example of this is found in Elvis Presley's "In the Ghetto." While its subject matter focuses on poor urban blacks, the point of view is clearly white, Christian, guilt-assuaging, and subtly patronizing; it tells us more about white, middle-class ideology than about how blacks live. The Clash's "White Riot" is not an apologia for the blacks, nor is it a fascistic defense of poor white youth's distrust of black immigrants. It sees the problem (not from a universal human, but) only from a white perspective (as the song is written and performed by a white group for white audiences), a viewpoint usually masked by the liberal projections at work in a song like

"In the Ghetto." Instead of a sentimental identification with or unconscious valorization of black culture/music, the Clash sees the two cultures as, at this stage, (due to education and cultural conditioning) separate but unequal. By comparing the white and black situations, working-class whites acquire a clearer view of their own dilemma. The white man can learn by seeing what he is not; black culture posits a lack in us as whites. "White Riot" is an essay addressed to us as the artist's peers. The essay states the problem as honestly as possible—but it is not a personal confession, or even a polemic (as Bob Dylan might have written). A later song of the Clash, "White Man in Hammersmith Palais," continues the meditation on the problem of two cultures and two musics co-existing in Britain.

In "Repetition," recorded in late 1977 by The Fall (a young Manchester group) the issue is extended to the *form* of rock music/punk rock music itself. While the content of punk is politically progressive, the music form seeks to eliminate progressive qualities in favor of basic rock and roll repetitions. Musical form (which then inevitably drifts back towards the "artistic" after its initial purge of these qualities) and the political content expressed by the lyrics are observed to be in contradiction with each other:

White noise / Look at them speeding / You don't wear a black and white tie / You're gonna make it on your own / Cause we dig you / Cause we dig you / Ah we dig you / Ah we dig you / Ah repetition of the drums and we're never gonna lose it. / This is the 3 R's: / Repetition / Repetition / Repetition . . . / Oh repetition in the music and we're never gonna lose it. / President Carter loves

repetition / Ah Chairman Mao he dug repetition / Oh repetition in China / Repetition in America / Repetition in West Germany / Simultaneous suicides / We dig it / We dig it . . .
From *Repetition* (The Fall).

THE HANDMADE READYMADE
DAVID DEITCHER

Shortly after Franz Kline's death in 1962, Elaine de Kooning wrote a catalogue essay for a memorial exhibition of his works. In it she told of a day, late in 1948, when Kline visited her and her husband, Willem. At the time Kline was anxious to find a way out of an impasse in his work. Two years after Jackson Pollock made his first "poured" paintings, at a time of continuing critical success for de Kooning and increased attention for other colleagues, Kline's work still consisted of easel paintings in a quasi-abstract style that at times seemed too reminiscent of de Kooning's own. De Kooning suggested to his friend that he take one of the ink sketches he had brought along and insert it into a Bell Opticon opaque projector that he had used to enlarge his own sketches onto canvas supports. Kline's epiphany occurred when he saw the image projected onto the studio wall:

A four by five inch brush drawing of a rocking chair . . . loomed in gigantic black strokes which eradicated any image, the strokes expanding as entities in themselves, unrelated to any reality but that of their own existence.[1]

From this procedure, which Kline would continue to use on and off for the rest of his life, there evolved the monumental paintings which, exhibited in 1950 at the Charles Egan Gallery, established his international reputation as a significant Abstract Expressionist.

Two years after that show, Harold Rosenberg published his famous essay, "The American Action Painters." In it he described such art as "a revolution against the given in the self and the world."[2] But in light of the reproductive procedure that Kline and de Kooning are known to have used from time to time, to what extent should such work be described in those terms? Since it is itself constituted of a "given" in the world, such a method of painting can be described as such a "revolution" in only the most qualified sense. That no one has allowed this fact to interfere in any significant way with the conventional interpretation of Abstract Expressionist art attests to the enduring appeal of such postwar cultural humanism. For a similar reason, the success of Pop Art had to occur before the special affection of Abstract Expressionists for American mass culture—cartoons, comics, and movies—could be considered as a valid element in understanding works like de Kooning's *Women*.[3]

Nevertheless, a greater willingness to consider the significance of such a re-presentional method might lead to a healthy skepticism regarding some of the commonplaces of expressionist ideology. For example, art critics and historians usually describe the relationship between Abstract Expressionist practice and the structural character of everyday life as one of fairly straightforward opposition. Yet, keeping Kline's procedure in mind, it seems more accurate to say that he *internal-*

ized the repetitive structure which dominates industrialized American life in order to stage more spectacularly his struggle against it. The idea that the action painter might have used reproductive means to assist him in a transcription which he then disguised beneath the ciphers of emphatic originality, makes it possible to describe such art not only as "original" (primarily in its goals and tactics) but also as a *dissimulated copy*. Moreover, consideration of this less familiar, even repressed, aspect of the action painter's method suggests that the relationship between Abstract Expressionism and the Pop Art that followed it was a more dialectical one than is commonly thought. That dialectic is evident in the way that Warhol, Lichtenstein and Oldenburg turned the Abstract Expressionists' order of priority on its head, and became the authors of *dissimulated originals*.

Dissimulation—in Pop's case, the production of originals that masquerade as copies—was not overlooked by critics of the new art, even some of the earliest ones. The paradoxical character of the Pop object was central to an unusually lively and revealing debate which took place in the art press late in 1963. Lichtenstein's earliest Pop paintings provoked this controversy, leading one critic to identify a completely new class of objects: the "handmade readymade." Brian O'Doherty (a.k.a. Patrick Ireland) coined the phrase "handmade readymade" in *The New York Times* when he reviewed Lichtenstein's second Pop show in New York. Labeling him "one of the worst artists in America," he nonetheless credited him with paintings that "raised some of the most difficult problems in art."[4]

O'Doherty cited the controversy concerning Lichtenstein's

work, since it had just erupted in the press. The September issues of both *Art News* and *Artforum* were running feature articles—one each—about Pop Art in general, and Lichtenstein's in particular. Both were written by an esteemed art instructor from California, Erle Loran, who had targeted two paintings by Roy Lichtenstein, *Portrait of Mme. Cézanne* and *Man with Folded Arms* (both 1962), in order to excoriate some of the more salient features of the new art.[5] Each painting was a characteristically brazen representation of a diagram from Loran's then twenty-year-old book, *Cézanne's Composition*. Loran, like O'Doherty, thought it absurd that so many supporters of Pop were defending Lichtenstein, in part, by insisting that he "transformed" rather than "copied" his sources. Claiming that only an expert could detect such transformation, O'Doherty found it all quite beside the point. After all, ever since 1913 it had been possible to classify *direct* appropriation as art. Marcel Duchamp, "the old master of innovation started it all by setting up his readymades . . . and calling them art, leaving on us the burden of proof that they were not." O'Doherty and Loran found the transformation alibi doubly annoying since it clinched the matter of Pop's high cultural status by facilitating a rather academic dual defense. On the one hand, it was art because it "put a frame of consciousness around a major part of American life . . . we take for granted, fulfilling a criterion students have been writing about in their notebooks for years." On the other, the fact that Lichtenstein transformed his sources "like a good artist should" fulfilled another commonplace of fine art. O'Doherty dismissed both lines of defense and, despairing of this "triumph of the banal," observed that "Mr. Lichtenstein's art is in the category, I suppose, of the handmade readymade."[6]

Loran wrote his two articles as a consequence of Lichtenstein's first Pop exhibition in Los Angeles, where the man-sized diagrammatic portrait of Cézanne's wife was on display. His articles may have marked a historical first: there is reason to believe that they displaced his desire to sue the artist and/or his dealer for copyright infringement—the first, though not the last, such litigious impulse to pepper the history of American art during and after the inception of Pop. The angrier of the two tracts appeared in *Art News*, where, in keeping with that magazine's editorial taste for human interest, Loran openly expressed his contempt for what he beheld and alluded to his desire to sue.

In a recent sell out exhibition at the Ferus Gallery, Los Angeles, he (Lichtenstein) gave the title of Portrait of Mme. Cézanne *to the black and white line drawing on bare canvas reproduced here. Sale price: $2,000, or more. I suppose I should be flattered that a diagrammatic sketch of mine should be worth so much. But then, no one has paid me anything—so far.*[7]

One does not have to read past the rhetorical question which served as Loran's title—"Pop Artists or Copy Cats?"—in order to detect what was most provocative about Lichtenstein's (and Warhol's) variety of Pop Art. Loran, like many other people, regarded Abstract Expressionism as a quintessentially American humanist art: a "monument to the human spirit," an emblem of the "depth and richness of human experience and intuition," and a demonstration of "the true meaning of free democracy . . . in America." He noted that

Abstract Expressionists had opened up new and unprecedented avenues for aesthetic exploration which Loran considered on a par with the "most advanced products of the human mind, comparable in some ways to achievements in physics and chemistry."[8] He was incensed that any self-respecting artist could possibly want to undermine so precious a cultural resource as Abstract Expressionism. That such a man would then be handsomely rewarded for advancing a culture of copies over one of originals was just too much for him to endure in silence.

Loran saw nothing significant in Pop "transformation." He insisted that Abstract Expressionists had ventured "far beyond the process of transforming nature" to produce paintings which presupposed "no conscious source but have an identity and imagery that is autonomous." He thereby argued that transformative activities could only amount to aesthetic regression.[9]

So insistently and so often was it said during the first year of Pop's critical reception that Lichtenstein "transformed" his sources—that his was not a repetition of Duchamp's dreaded gesture—that the artist himself felt obliged to offer his own cogent, laconic corrective. Shortly after the publication of Loran's two articles (the second of which was entitled, notably "Cézanne and Lichtenstein: Problems of Transformation"), Lichtenstein responded to one of Gene Swenson's questions by stating: "Transformation is a strange word to use. It implies that art transforms. It doesn't, it just plain forms."[10]

Among the critics who joined Loran in his assault, Max Kozloff was sufficiently disturbed by "this little event" in the art press to devote an entire article to it. In the pages of *The*

Nation he concluded that art like Lichtenstein's signaled something not so little after all: "a rejection of the deepest values of modern art."[11] When Kozloff noted that for six or seven years in New York, "we have been witnessing an attack upon the notion of originality in painting," he pinpointed both the central feature of the Loran controversy, and the crucial normative term within the modernist system of aesthetic evaluation which Pop placed in jeopardy. He too feared the implications that this attack upon artistic invention would have for "the ethic of most twentieth-century art." Kozloff condemned work like Lichtenstein's and Warhol's for depending on the high art "context" for its effect; without the art context, he postulated, such objects would revert back to their status as non-art. Pop Art was, in his words, "as contextual as it is conceptual," an observation which would seem to situate Pop within the tradition of the "historical avant-garde" to the extent that such art prompts a critical reflexivity regarding the institutional framework of art. But this observation does not take into account the singularly contradictory character of the handmade readymade, without which the entire debate about transformation would not have occurred, and which secured Pop's place within the realm of "neo-avant-garde" practice.[12]

This paradoxical form imposed limits upon American Pop's critique of earlier aesthetic practices, but the emergence of monumental handpainted or silkscreened ads and comic book images forced many observers to admit and reflect upon the gradual erosion of the Abstract Expressionist paradigm. The authority of Abstract Expressionist aesthetics had depended upon the viability of the interrelated concepts of stylistic authenticity and metaphorical structure, as well as the mythic notion of the autonomous creator. That these concepts had become, at best, contestible and, at worst, discredited, was apparent when Kozloff observed that since the mid-1950s "there grew a cleavage between the motivating idea and its embodiment, the fusion of which had been the guiding premise of Abstract Expression."[13] This "cleavage" corresponds with the dissolution of the symbolic mode of address and the loss of the attendant metaphoric conception of a transparency between style and the artist, and it had been evident in the anomalous practices of Robert Rauschenberg (i.e., *Erased de Kooning*, 1953), and Jasper Johns (*Target with Four Faces*, 1955). This is another way of saying that a split had opened between form and content, upon whose fusion Abstract Expressionists depended, not just for their metaphoric conception of style, but for their claim to descendance from an aesthetic tradition which arguably could be traced to the birth of humanism. That the Pop object could be described as a *handmade* readymade offered little solace to the American defenders of aesthetic autonomy.

Looking at Pop also prompted the realization that the once crucial distinction between abstraction and representation was "no longer relevant." Even for artists who, unlike Kline and de Kooning, might never have taken recourse to mechanical devices whose effect was to transform abstractions into representations, abstract imagery had become encoded, recognizable.

. . . it is quite as possible to put comic strips through their mechanistic paces as it is concentric circles. In fact, as conventionalized icons they ultimately have about equivalent non-meanings . . . this phase

146

in art opposes the straightforwardness of its predecessor with subterfuge.[14]

One cannot very well sustain a view of a modernist vanguard as the last resolutely unique object in the midst of a commodity culture dominated by equivalence once the artistic image joins all others in its failure to establish the illusory union between form and content that testifies to its transcendent status. Once the pictorial signifier cannot be counted on to fuse with its intended signified, it achieves parity only with other signifiers as one side of a now irretrievably fractured relationship to the signified. In this sense all images had acquired an equivalence with one another in their capacity to yield "non-meaning."

When artists like Warhol and Lichtenstein challenged the goals of Abstract Expressionists, they benefited enormously from the gulf that had opened up between pictorial signifier and signified. Concerning style, Warhol could note, "I think that would be so great, to be able to change styles. And I think that's what's going to happen, that's going to be the whole new scene."[15] One effect of such a dislocation of style from its former congruence with the concept of authenticity is that it problematized the matter of locating the voice of the "author" as was never possible under the old and once durable order of metaphor. The Pop object is neither metaphoric nor metonymic; stripped of any symbolic function, it has no depth. As Roland Barthes observed, no artist can be found "behind" this obdurate object. Confronted by it, he was moved to recall a "true revolution of language."[16]

To the extent that the aesthetic practices associated with

Pop, and with earlier works by Johns and Rauschenberg, can be described in terms of the dissolution of metaphor, it is not surprising that they heralded the corresponding return to prominence of allegorical procedures. According to Walter Benjamin's pioneering work on allegory, the allegorist appropriates images (or objects) in a seemingly arbitrary fashion, thus severing them from their original function and meaning. Such appropriation recontextualizes the image, situating it within another network of signifying relations; as Benjamin said: "This meaning with that image, that image with this meaning." The signifier, its original signified now isolated, is able simultaneously to produce a new meaning that is potentially antithetical to the old.[17] This structural fact of allegory had great significance for Pop artists, enabling them to deploy images that could function, on the one hand, at the level of the most debased mass cultural sign (the comic strip referent) while, on the other, insisting upon its exalted status as high art (the comic strip panel of a jet plane exploding functions—for some—as a critical cipher of Abstract Expressionism). The handmade readymade is the perfect vehicle for the contradictory messages embedded within works of Pop Art. Consequently, Pop Art was able to assume a uniquely conciliatory social function which was the key to its unprecedented popular and institutional success.

Pop Art secured a vast, socially diversified audience for art, while allowing the more privileged among its ranks the "distinguished" aesthetic response which had been their birthright since the origins of modernism.[18] Warhol understood that Pop Art would attract greater numbers of spectators from more diverse social backgrounds into the hitherto exclusive spaces of high art, and he also knew that they would not all understand it in the same way.

The young people who know about it will be the people who are more intelligent and know about art. But the people who don't know about art would like it better because it is what they know ... the people who really like art don't like the art now, while the people who don't know about art like what we are doing.[19]

The conciliatory function of Pop was also evident in the fact that these artists could resolve the normative pairs of discursive terms—unique/reproduced, original/copy, high culture/mass culture—whose hitherto rigorously maintained antagonism had preserved the integrity of high culture and the latter's legitimizing social effect.

As early as 1962 Donald Judd recognized this potential when he reviewed Lichtenstein's first Pop show and, after noting the contradictory character of his paintings, ruminated upon their broader cultural effect. He quickly tempered what might have seemed disagreeable about Lichtenstein's works—their proximity to the stylistic codes and content of mass culture—by noting the "traditional" and "quite expert" composition of works like *The Kiss*. Then he added:

Respectability comes quickly, is strong and can be shrewd. Lichtenstein's comics and advertisements destroy the necessity to which the usual definitions pretend.[20]

149

This enigmatic comment refers to Lichtenstein's ability to navigate his way successfully through the minefield of high and low cultural terms. By representing the mass cultural artifact, while (trans)forming it in such a way that the new object skillfully dissimulates its traditional aesthetic rewards, Lichtenstein could indeed "destroy the necessity to which the usual definition (i.e. between "high" and "low" culture, between original and copy, etc.) pretends." In this way Pop artists meddled with the normative terms by which high art and mass culture had once been kept apart.

Such meddling was one of the self-professed goals of Pop artists. This was evident in a 1964 conversation between Andy Warhol, Claes Oldenburg and Roy Lichtenstein in which they discussed this and other related matters. Oldenburg noted that he had "always been bothered by distinctions—that this is good and this is bad and this is better."

I am especially bothered by the distinction between commercial and fine art, or between fine painting and accidental effects. I think we have made a deliberate attempt to explore this area . . .

Oldenburg was interested in parody, dissimulation, and how they enabled him to explore the differences between, for example, a sculpture by Arp and some spilled ketchup. He noted that by making things that looked as much as possible like the prosaic original, he was able, paradoxically, "to emphasize my art and the arbitrary act of the artist who can bring it into relief somehow."[21] Lichtenstein underscored another crucial aspect of the Pop artist's agenda when, responding to a comment about the impersonality of his and Warhol's art, he took issue with that widespread tendency—born of the numbing effects of life in an advanced consumer culture—to assume that "similar things are identical."

Since the structure of the handmade readymade insured an experience of ontological difference in perception between the Pop object and the mass cultural one—between a Warhol can of *Campbell's Soup* and Campbell's own—it was able to preserve a vestige of the action painter's "revolution against the given in the self and in the world."[22] Coming after the war, during the boom years of the early-1960's consumer culture, Pop artists ceded "invention" in order to preserve an essential effect of idealist modernism. In fact, the *raison d'être* for all art which has followed Jasper Johns's crucial precedent by attracting the spectator's attention to a target—or a map, a beer can, or all "things the mind already knows"—has been steadfastly to oppose this most commonplace form of memory in a concrete perception of a subtle, yet symbolically significant difference. Recognition of the sort that is triggered by popular images is the equal of the "voluntary memory" that Marcel Proust found so deficient when, early in this century, he tried to recapture an elusive experiential fullness and unity in his monumental novel, *A la recherche du temps perdus*. Since the early 19th century, voluntary memory has been one of the perennial objects of historical processes the aim of which has been to colonize human beings, body and soul; today advertising is its most ubiquitous, highly developed manifestation.[23] Pop artists could thus salvage the utopian modernist tradition—staged more immediately by Abstract Expressionists under profoundly different cultural circumstances—of opposing the effects of industrialized life within the elaborately sanctioned, imaginary spaces of discrete works of art.

What, precisely, has Erle Loran's contribution to American cultural history been? Between 1936 and 1981 he was a professor of art at the University of California, Berkeley. That is to say, he belonged to the same generation, possessed the same type of institutional affiliation, and shared many of the same pedagogical goals as those American art instructors who, during the 1940s, introduced the majority of the artists we associate with Pop to the technical skills and belief systems which they considered indispensable to good modern art and design. This generation of art educators shared the common goal of spreading the gospel of modernism to unprecedented numbers of people in the U.S. When Loran published *Cézanne's Composition* in 1943, his goal was to disclose the fundamental principles of pictorial organization as the latter are evident in Cézanne's art.

In his book, Loran had noted several earlier contributions to such an attempt to divulge the secrets of "space composition," earliest among them, Adolf Hildebrand's *The Problem of Form in Painting and Sculpture* (1893) and, closer to home, Thomas Hart Benton's essay, "Mechanics of Form Organization in Painting" (1926-27). The illustrations which Benton used in his essay— abstract diagrams which anticipated the all-over compositional schema in paintings like Jackson Pollock's *Mural* (1943)— suggested to Loran the pedagogical value of using diagrams in his book.[24] He placed these compositional maps, based on specific works by Cézanne, next to reproductions of the latter. These he juxtaposed in the pages of his book with photographs of the artist's original motifs.

The resulting comparative method made it possible for Loran to lead the reader, as systematically and with as little doubt as possible, through the intricacies of Cézanne's compositional logic. Cézanne's art was to be laid bare, its significance assessed entirely in terms of formal logic. Loran's diagrams were the kind that connote scientific method, and which were often used during the 1940s and '50s for the less than scientific purpose of instructing people in "creative," leisure-time activities. In this sense, they are similar to those images which Andy Warhol pictured in his paintings, *Dance Diagram—Fox Trot* and *Dance Diagram—Tango* (1961, 1962). Along with his series entitled *Do it Yourself* (1962), and Lichtenstein's monumentalized how-to-Cézannes, these works comprise a distinct and historically allusive genre within early Pop: a parody of images that should be associated with the popularization of high culture in the U.S.

Cézanne's Composition is in many ways itself a vintage '40s object, a manifestation of that highly significant, far-reaching, and too rarely noted attempt in the U.S. to extend the benefits of cultural activities in general, and of modernist art in particular, to ever larger, more socially diverse numbers of Americans *before* as well as after World War II. It was largely due to the successful results of that attempt (whose roots can be traced to the activities of the W.P.A.) that Clement Greenberg addressed himself when, in 1947, he reiterated the terms of his nearly decade-old argument (first outlined in his 1939 essay, "Avant-Garde and Kitsch") that, if high culture was to survive in the postwar era, American artists would have to produce the kind of radically abstract, anti-domestic, and decidedly elitist art which Jackson Pollock and his Abstract Expressionist colleagues had then begun to exhibit in New York. As Greenberg put it, a new class of patrons was "surging toward culture under the pressure of anxiety, high taxes, and a shrinking industrial frontier." These individuals

Would demand cultural goods that are up to date and yet not too hard to consume ... This state of affairs constitutes a much greater threat to high art than Kitsch itself ... The future of art and literature will brighten in this country only when a new cultural elite appears with enough consciousness to counterbalance the pressure of the new mass market.[25]

Loran's book had managed to unite Alfred Barr, Thomas Craven and Clement Greenberg, among others, in their high regard for what the latter described in the pages of *The Nation* as a "more essential" understanding of Cézanne's art than any other he had encountered in print.[26] Although Loran's book was specialized, technically sophisticated, and rather high-minded, it was nevertheless a product of the drive to evolve more systematic and scientific methods of teaching the fundamentals of modernist pictorial construction to increasing numbers of art students. Many of them later would go on to join that "surge" toward culture which Greenberg had found so threatening. Others became Pop artists.

Of Pop artists it can truly be said that they were among the first generation of American artists to be professionally educated in university art departments, or in fully accredited, degree-granting art schools. Moreover, they experienced a unique moment in the history of American modernist art instruction when a singularly rational—one might even say "rationalized"—approach to teaching the skills of fine art and design united with a powerfully romantic belief in the inherent beneficiality of art and science. The efficient pedagogical methods by which Lichtenstein and Warhol were taught endowed both artists with that mastery of paradox which so frequently has been detected in their mature work. The conjunction of a demystifying, often positivistic approach to art training with an ongoing, romantic belief in art's conciliatory, restorative powers constitutes an important historical precedent, a structural analogue for the Pop artist's paradoxical aesthetic procedure, and for its ultimate product, the "handmade readymade."

Notes:

1) Elaine de Kooning, "Franz Kline: Painter of His Own Life," *Art News*, vol. 61, November 1962, p. 68. Reprinted from exhibition catalogue, *Franz Kline* (Washington Gallery of Modern Art, Washington, D.C., 1962).

2) Harold Rosenberg, "The American Action Painters," reprinted in *The Tradition of the New* (Chicago, University of Chicago Press, 1982), p. 32.

3) For an example of the increased receptivity of critics after the birth of Pop to the importance of mass cultural interests among Abstract Expressionists, see Thomas B. Hess's text in the exhibition catalogue: *Willem de Kooning* (New York, Museum of Modern Art, 1968), esp. p. 76 ff. There Hess noted the artist's complaint that nobody had noticed how funny the "Women" really were; with traditional art historical logic, Hess then claimed these paintings as a "direct influence" on Pop artists. For an analysis of Kline's involvement with popular culture, see Albert Boime, "Franz Kline and the Figurative Tradition," (cat. essay) *Franz Kline: The Early Work as Signals* (S.U.N.Y., Binghamton, 1977). There he cited Elaine de Kooning's story of Kline's self-discovery through opaque projection, which Boime described (p. 17) as follows: "The process of magnification had a double meaning for Kline: it monumentalized his work and simultaneously legitimized it in his eyes through its analogy with the movies' primitive ancestor, the comic strip." In keeping with the image of Abstract Expressionists as

cultural descendants of Prometheus, Boime understood this to "foreshadow Lichtenstein's and the photorealists' more mechanical amplification of images."

4) Brian O'Doherty, "Doubtful but Definite Triumph of the Banal," *The New York Times*, October 27, 1963, Section 2, p. 21.

5) Erle Loran, "Cézanne and Lichtenstein: Problems of Transformation," *Artforum*, vol. 2, September 1963, pp. 34-35; "Pop Artists or Copy Cats?," *Art News*, vol. 62, September 1963, pp. 48-49, 61.

6) O'Doherty, op.cit.

7) Loran, *Art News*, p. 48.

8) Loran, *Artforum*, p. 35.

9) Ibid.

10) Gene Swenson, "What is Pop Art?" (Interviews with Eight Painters, Part I), *Art News*, vol. 62, no. 7, November 1963; reprinted in John Coplans, ed. *Roy Lichtenstein* (New York, Praeger Publishers, 1972), p. 53.

11) Max Kozioff, "Art," *The Nation*, vol. 197, November 2, 1963, p. 284.

12) Ibid., p. 285. The terms, "historical avant-garde" and "neo-avant-garde," were first used in this sense by Peter Bürger. Historical avant-gardism refers to those works of Dada, Russian Constructivism and Productivism, and Surrealism which Bürger understood to challenge the institutionalized concept of autonomous art; works which attempted to "integrate (art) into the praxis of life." He used the term "neo-avant-garde" to account for those forms of art which, after World War II, reiterate historical avant-gardist procedures, the criticality of which has been foreclosed as a result, on the one hand, of the institutionalization of the avant-garde and, on the other, the "false sublation" of art into everyday life which results from the voraciousness of a consumer culture that has extended the logic of the commodity into every area of life. See Peter Bürger, *Theory of the Avant-Garde*, trans. Michael Shaw (University of Minnesota Press, 1984).

13) Kozloff, op. cit., p. 285.

14) Ibid., p. 285.

15) Andy Warhol, quoted in Gene Swenson, "What is Pop Art?" reprinted in John Russell, Suzi Gablik, *Pop Art Redefined* (London, Thames and Hudson, 1969), p. 117.

16) Roland Barthes, "That Old Thing, Art . . ." in this volume. In 1968 Barthes had already disccussed the "revolution in language" which he recalled in this essay more extensively. See: "The Death of the Author," in Roland Barthes, *Image-Music-Text*, ed. trans. by Stephen Heath (New York, Hill and Wang, 1977), p. 142 ff.

17) Walter Benjamin quoted in Benjamin H.D. Buchloh, "Allegorical Procedures: Appropriation and Montage in Contemporary Art," *Artforum*, vol. 11, no. 1, September 1982, p. 46.

18) On the concept of "distinction" as used here, see Pierre Bourdieu, *Distinction: A Social Critique of the Judgement of Taste*, trans. Richard Nice (Cambridge Mass., Harvard University Press, 1984).

19) Warhol quoted in Bruce Glaser, "Oldenburg, Lichtenstein, Warhol: A Discussion," reprinted in Coplans, op. cit., p. 65.

20) Donald Judd, "Roy Lichtenstein," *Arts Magazine*, April, 1962, p. 52.

21) Glaser, op. cit., p. 62.

22) Warhol's work has often been described as if it were the fulfilment of his oft-quoted, and as frequently misunderstood, observation that, "everybody should be a machine." There is a considerable difference between a Warhol image (or object) and the thing it represents, and that difference is an aesthetic one. The difference between Warhol's aesthetic (trans) formations and Lichtenstein's—so often contrasted with each other to claim that Warhol's is no aesthetic at all or, at best, an "anti-aesthetic"—is that Lichtenstein's are traditionally aesthetic. The idea that Warhol's art is virtually devoid of aesthetic "information" can be put to rest if one is willing to recognize as aesthetic his deliberately informal, usually off-register silkscreen method, his garish use of color, and, above all, his discovery that seriality can function as *both* composition and expressive device. Rather, the aesthetic character of Warhol's work seems invisible to spectators because it is distilled so completely from mass culture and advertising, resources which some observers, their outlook either modernist, anti-modernist, or a paradoxical, some-times puritanical combination of both, shun.

23) The colonization of memory and its connection to the history of drawing instruction and general education are discussed in my "Drawing from Memory," (cat. essay) *The Art of Memory: The Loss of History* (New York, The New Museum of Contemporary Art, 1985), pp. 15-21.

24) Erle Loran, *Cézanne's Composition* (Berkeley, University of California Press, 1943; reprint, 1963), p. 3.

25) Clement Greenberg, "The Present Prospects of American Painting and Sculpture." *Horizon*, nos. 93-94, October 1947, p. 22. Reprinted in John O'Brien, ed., *Clement Greenberg: The Collected Essays and Criticism*, (Chicago, University of Chicago Press, 1986), vol. 2, p. 160 ff.

26) Clement Greenberg, "Cézanne's Composition by Earle (sic) Loran," *The Nation*, December 29, 1945; reprinted in O'Brian, vol. II, p. 47.

CAPITAL PICTURES
MARY ANNE STANISZEWSKI

Pop Art makes capital visible. Modernism produced autonomous high culture, the avant-garde attacked this tradition,[1]
and American Pop Art since the early Sixties has represented
exchange value—the principle that creates the meaning and
worth of everything in a capitalist system. With the possible
exception of currency itself, art as we know it—that is, art since
the late 18th century—may be the clearest model of the
workings of capital. This fundamental but implicit feature of
art came into full view in the 1960s when Andy Warhol, James
Rosenquist and Roy Lichtenstein translated the abstracted
sovereignty of exchange value—the power of money—into
painted pictures.

Art has no inherent use value. Aesthetic criteria in the
modern era are not utilitarian. The significance of art is created
by its circulation within an economy made up of exhibition in
galleries, ownership by patrons, endorsement by critics, canon-
ization in art history, and reproduction within the mass media.
Modern art has traditionally been resistant to easy assimilation
within the institutional frameworks that invest it with meaning and value. In the United States in the early Sixties, fine art's
marginal relation to the economic apparatus, for the most

part, dissolved; the mechanisms for its smooth reception and marketing consolidated; and its relatively latent function as a commodity became dominant. Pop is the dialectical moment when art changes: no longer mythically outside the system as aestheticized modernism nor an instrument deployed with subversive intent, art is institutionalized as fuel for the cultural and economic machinery while serving as one of capitalism's most self-reflexive representations. The unprecedented reception of this work is testimony to the location of value in late capitalism—in celebrity and money.[2]

Pop Art is the crystallization of culture industry—a social formation that took several decades to consolidate and within whose legacy all contemporary art functions. Beginning in the late 1930s, in a body of diverse but related art criticism and social theory, the signs of the culture industry were recognized and its contours were drawn. At about the same time—from the Thirties through the Fifties—this phenomenon was gradually taking institutional form at the Museum of Modern Art. By the early Sixties, in the United States, the art object itself became a mirror of culture industry. Pop Art is important because it provides an image of the character and contradictions of late capitalism. And equally significant is Pop Art's reception—its actual social life, that is, its assimilation by galleries and museums, its appraisal by the critical and historical communities and its reproduction within the mass media. Pop's circulation within the system was and continues to be one of the most emblematic demonstrations of capital as realized in the culture industry.

When Walter Benjamin (writing in Paris in 1936) observed a change in the function of the work of art in the age of mechanical reproduction, he was reasoning from an avant-gardist perspective. Benjamin envisioned the mass media emancipating art from its ritualistic and cult value, transforming it into an instrument for political and social change. In 1944, however, the Frankfurt School theorists Theodor Adorno and Max Horkheimer (who had been colleagues of Benjamin and were writing in exile in California) criticized the increasing absorption of all aspects of western society within a consumer-oriented mass media and entertainment business. They described this development as "culture industry." Adorno's and Horkheimer's ideas resembled the well-known criticism of Clement Greenberg. In 1939-1940, Greenberg had warned that art was becoming indistinguishable from mass-produced culture and kitsch. But Adorno and Horkheimer specifically aligned the commodification of the modern world with the increasing domination of exchange value. They recognized that use value, the utility of a commodity, is not determined by natural law but is created by exchange within the marketplace. Lamenting the loss of any pretense of inherent use value which had existed in earlier moments of capitalism, Adorno and Horkheimer argued that all essentialist relationships within signification and existence had dissolved. Where art in the modern era had previously resisted its status as a commodity, it was now becoming nothing more than a luxury good. For Adorno and Horkheimer, "The whole world is made to pass through the filter of culture industry," and they saw before them an "age of universal publicity" where everything is appropriated for mechanical reproduction and where a fetishism of exchange value and consumerism is the order of the day.[3]

In France, similar ideas gained currency in the work of the Marxist sociologist Henri Lefebvre who, in the Forties, began to deal with the commodification of modern life. In the Fifties and the Sixties, he specifically criticized the loss of faith in symbolic meanings derived from nature. Lefebvre described a post-World War II world where signification was determined by convention, a culture he characterized in 1968 as "The Bureaucratic Society of Controlled Consumption." Lefebvre had an important impact upon French Situationists like Guy Debord whose aphoristic *Society of the Spectacle* (1967) most simply and clearly describes this "inverted reality" where exchange value determines use and where "the commodity had attained the *total occupation* of the social life." Debord visualized this phenomenon "in the limited sense of the 'mass media' " and made the key formulation that "The spectacle is *capital* to such a degree of accumulation that it becomes an image."[4]

The Museum of Modern Art can serve as a paradigm for the institutionalization of culture industry, illustrating its development, its complexities and its contradictions.[5] From MoMA's inception in 1929 through the Fifties, the museum implemented what might be described as modern art's absorption within a Situationist's spectacle, by staging—perhaps to an even greater degree than Greenberg or Adorno and Horkheimer imagined—culture's transformation into the fine art of publicity. The museum produced exhibitions within the extremes of a spectrum which spanned from painting and sculpture shows to exhibits that attempted to break down the boundaries between art and everyday life. MoMA's history during these years is the history of the assimilation of modernist and avant-garde practices within an institutional framework.

The museum's programs, however, demonstrate the inadequacy of neatly defining modernism and the historical avant-garde. Many of MoMA's exhibitions were hybrid and had contradictory agendas. The 1949 "Modern Art in Your Life" compared the forms found in modern art with the commonplace objects of the modern world. For example, in the "Abstract Geometric Form" section, the high modernist paintings of Mondrian were seen in relation to a wall unit of storage shelves and a box of Kleenex Tissues. The 1934 "Machine Art" show served as a course in good modern design, but the entries—which ranged from kitchen sinks to ball bearings—were displayed as if they were purely aesthetic objects.

The museum appropriated avant-garde tactics in order to educate the American audience and to integrate the innovations of modern art into society. MoMA's early years illustrate the variety of purposes and politics these strategies have served. Different from the traditional history that places avant-garde projects within predominantly critical or leftist practices, the museum exemplifies the absorption of these methods and innovations within a capitalist system MoMA functioned as an instrument of America's dominant ideology, in many instances proliferating images of liberal democracy and working closely with city and federal governments.

"Good Design" shows were initiated in 1938. Composed of common household objects—pots, pans, brooms, silverware—these exhibitions were intended to educate the consumer but they also increased the sales of the displayed products, which led manufacturers to vie for museum appro-val.[6] In the Forties, exhibitions like the "Road to Victory" or the "Magazine Cover Competition: Women in Necessary Civilian Employment" contributed to the war effort. And the appropriation of American abstract painting as an instrument of the Cold War has been documented.[7] The museum became a cultural production house serving American government, industry, business and foreign policy.

The diversity of exhibitions found at MoMA during its first three decades is very different from what we find at the museum today. Consider the year spanning 1953-1954: post-war cars, including a Porsche, a Studebaker and an MG, were showcased in the "Ten Autmobiles" show of September 1953. A Léger painting exhibition opened in October. The annual Holiday Carnival turned the museum galleries into a creative play-space for children at Christmas time. And in March 1954, "Signs in the Street" filled the first floor gallery and garden terrace with signs and photographs of signs from highways, bus stops, gas stations and buildings. The "Signs in the Street" press release describes the exhibition as "the aspect of daily life"[8] most recently surveyed by the Museum of Modern Art. The sculpture garden—filled with this collection of Pop signs—looked as if it were a three-dimensional prototype of a Pop Art painting. At the show's entrance a photo-mural of Fifth Avenue was installed—"a typical example of the chaos of signs in our streets."[9] In the mid-Fifties the museum visitor could drift from gallery to gallery experiencing the pleasures of abstract art in one room and the simulated chaos of our streets in the next. Overall, the museum's agenda involved preserving the integrity of an aestheticized modernism while deploying avant-garde methods to integrate high art into the social fabric. In the mid-Fifties, however, MoMA was creating a spectacle simulating the variety and seduction of the modern world's visual array. The museum became the place where both a Léger painting and a Shell gas station sign were offered for aesthetic consumption.

With regard to Pop, the Museum of Modern Art is forgotten history; the exhibitions that took place in London during the Fifties are much more familiar. It was within the context of discussion groups, lectures and exhibitions held at London's Institute of Contemporary Art and the Whitechapel Art Gallery that the term Pop—meaning popular culture—first gained currency.[10] These several shows shared the Museum of Modern Art's agenda to present an all-embracing diversity of visual experience. The 1956 exhibition "This is Tomorrow" held at the Whitechapel Art Gallery is perhaps the best known. Lawrence Alloway in the catalogue introduction described it as "a lesson in spectatorship."[11] Twelve distinct exhibits incorporated popular culture and abstract art within architecturally designed pavilions. According to Alloway, "'This is Tomorrow' was not dealing with reforming society or presenting idealized industrial forms, but was an attempt to re-create the visual activity of the city scape, the street, carnivals, crowds and fashion."[12]

What was taking place in London and at the Museum of Modern Art in the Fifties was the organization of the culture industry. The diverse array of contemporary culture was on display for visual consumption and, in a sense was actualizing, in exhibition form, Adorno and Horkheimer's premise that "The whole world is made to pass through the filter of culture

165

industry." This transformation of exhibition entries into sheer visual spectacle was Pop—a phenomenon that was critically reproduced in the paintings of Andy Warhol, James Rosenquist and Roy Lichtenstein in the early Sixties.

The work of these three painters during these years should be distinguished from the vast array of art that falls under the rubric of Pop. Their painting does not merely incorporate or reproduce commodities or pop culture; it represents the strategies as well as the seduction of the mass media which generates consumption.[13] The critical distance of this work can be seen by comparing Warhol's commercial art of the Fifties with his Pop Art of the Sixties. In 1957, Warhol's portraits of movie stars cast as shoes were featured in a *Life* magazine picture story.[14] One of these reproductions, the Elvis Presley—a buccaneer boot with gold trimming—is a sketch made by a fan who located stardom's fetishism in the glamour of fashion. In 1962, Warhol was still fascinated by movie stars and obsessively making pictures of Elvis Presley but he had radically relocated the source of his desire. Silkscreening Elvis freeze frames in multiples as part of a series of nearly identical paintings, he simulated the repetition of reproduction that engenders celebrity. In the Fifties sketch, the artist's fetishism was directed at Elvis Presley; in the Sixties it is redirected to the system of repetition and exchange that creates cultural codes. In the Elvis series, Warhol illustrated that stars are born within the same abstracted domain where the meanings and values of society are created.

Rosenquist explained his work in 1964: "If I use a lamp or a chair, that isn't the subject . . . the relationships may be the subject matter, the relationships of the fragments I do. The

content will be something more gained from the relationships
... One thing, though, the subject matter isn't popular images,
it isn't that at all."[15] In Rosenquist's larger-than-life-size sur-
real montages—his *President Elect* (1960-1961) or *I Love
You With My Ford* (1961)—his subject is not simply the cars,
the trademarks, the women or the food, rather it is the
abstracted relation between these reproduced image-
fragments. In his *Marilyn Monroe* (1962) the image-
fragments of the movie star's face are superimposed upon
those of the Coca-Cola trademark. The brand name and the
public image clearly demonstrate the cultural contingency of
representation. A trademark or brand name has no inherent
bond to its referent—it functions to distinguish one virtually
identical product from another. A public image similarly
acquires meaning and exists exclusively within the stream of
reproductions that produces an arbitrary code of differences.
The "economy" that creates meaning also creates desire for
these products and celebrities. Rosenquist's paintings trans
cribe into a single image the abstracted flow of the mass media
that fuels our society of consumption.

Warhol, Rosenquist and Lichtenstein synthetically took
into account the process in which their "sources" were constituted: their images bear evidence of being mediated through
mechanical reproduction. The Warhols are photo-silkscreens,
Rosenquist's image-fragments are painted reproductions. In
Lichtenstein's paintings, color, shading and line—traditionally
understood and deployed as vehicles for the artist's subjective
expression—are organized within standardized codes. His
colors are unvarying commercial red, blue and yellow, his
shading is signified through the printers' code of Ben Day dots,

and his line eschews all personal character. This is in contrast to the work of Jasper Johns where the artist ironically inscribed his expressionistic brushstrokes within recognizable signs, symbols and clichés while he exaggerated the materiality and tactile quality. This is very different from the absence of facture and the seemingly or actually mass-produced execution found in the work of Johns's three successors.

This Sixties American Pop Art should also be distinguished from the "proto-Pop" collages and combines of Johns and Robert Rauschenberg and that of the Europeans Richard Hamilton and Eduardo Paolozzi. In the paintings of Warhol, Rosenquist and Lichtenstein, there are (with rare exceptions) no collages, no actual mass-produced fragments and no found objects. There are none of the damaged goods which were so prevalent during the Fifties and Sixties in the art of assemblage or *art brut*. Different from the withering away of the industrial object, all kinds of commodities, works of art and currencies are resurrected in these paintings within a simulated spectacle of reproduction. Pop represents the language of images circulated within the mass media where all sense of origin and concrete substance dissolves. It is the abstracted domain of capital translated into marketable pictures.

Notes:
1) I am using these terms as outlined in Peter Bürger's *Theory of the Avant-Garde*, foreward J. Schulte-Sasse, trans. M. Shaw, Minneapolis, 1984, where modernism is aestheticized autonomous art and the historical avant-garde of the Teens through the Thirties is distinguished by the recognition of the institution of modern art and is characterized by attempts to integrate art into the fabric of everyday life. Although the formulation is helpful in laying a foundation for understanding modern art, much of

20th-century art cannot be so simply categorized. The majority of the projects were complex and hybrid: consider Piet Mondrian's paintings within the De Stijl avant-garde.

2) No art produced by contemporary living artists has been deemed as "valuable" as Pop Art. It exhibits the returns of high yield investment: the 1973 Scull Collection sale was the landmark auction that publically demonstrated contemporary art's cash value. The sale total was $2,232,900. The first time a contemporary artwork hit the million dollar figure was Jasper Johns's *Three Flags* (1958) in 1980—the painting originally sold for $900. And in 1987, Rosenquist's *F-111* (1965) was the largest painting ever to come up at auction and its price, $2,090,000, was almost 100 times the amount the artist was paid in 1965.

3) Walter Benjamin, "The Work of Art in the Age of Mechanical Reproduction," *Illuminations*, ed. and intro. H. Arendt, trans. H. Zohn, New York, 1978, pp. 217-251, originally published "L'oeuvre d'art à l'époque de sa reproduction mécanisée," *Zeitschrift für Sozialforschung* 5, Paris, 1936. Theodor W. Adorno and Max Horkheimer, "The Culture Industry: Enlightenment as Mass Deception," *Dialectic of Enlightenment*, trans. J. Cumming, New York 1972, pp. 120-167, originally published, *Dialektik der Aufklärung*, New York, 1944. Clement Greenberg, "Avant-Garde and Kitsch," and "Towards a Newer Laocoon," *The Collected Essays and Criticism: vol. 1: Perceptions and Judgments 1939-1944*, ed. O'Brian, pp. 5-22 and 23-38, originally published *Partisan Review* 6, Fall 1939 and 7, July-August 1940.

4) Henri Lefebvre, *Everyday Life in the Modern World*, intro. P. Wander, trans. S. Rabinovitch, New Brunswick, New Jersey and London, 1984. Lefebvre had planned to write three volumes of *Critique de la vie quotidienne*. In 1947 he published the first volume with the subtitle, *Introduction*. Volume II was published in 1961 with the subtitle *Fondements d'une sociologie de la quotidienneté* and a précis of a projected third volume entitled *La vie quotidienne dans la monde moderne* was published in 1968 and was first translated into English by S. Rabinovitch in 1971. Guy Debord's, *Society of the Spectacle*, Detroit, 1983 was originally published *La Société du spectacle*, Paris, 1967.

5) Christopher Phillips' "The Judgment Seat of Photography," *October* 22, Fall 1982, pp. 27-63, is the key text dealing with one aspect of the museum's exhibition history.

6) Russell Lynes, *Good Old Modern: An Intimate Portrait of the Museum of Modern Art*, New York, 1973, pp. 180-181.

7) See Eva Cockcroft, "Abstract Expressionism: Weapon of the Cold War," *Artforum*, June 1974, pp. 39-41; Max Kozloff, "American Painting during the Cold War," *Artforum*, May 1973, pp. 42-54; Serge Guilbaut, "The New Adventures of the Avant-Garde in America," *October 15*, Winter 1980, pp. 61-78 and *How New York Stole the Idea of Modern Art: Abstract Expressionism, Freedom and the Cold War*, trans. A. Goldhammer, Chicago and London, 1943.

8) The Museum of Modern Art Press Release, March 23, 1954.

9) Ibid.

10) For a discussion of London and the history of the Pop situation see Dick Hebdige, "In Poor Taste: Notes on Pop," in this volume, and Anne Massey and Penny Sparke, "The Myth of the Independent Group," *Block* 10, 1985, pp. 48-55.

11) Lawrence Alloway, *This is Tomorrow*, Whitechapel Art Gallery, London, 1956, p. 2.

12) Lawrence Alloway, "The Development of British Pop," in Lucy Lippard, *Pop Art*, New York and Washington, 1968, pp. 27-67.

13) This reading of Pop has been informed by the writings of Jean Baudrillard. For an analysis of Pop Art that foregrounds Baudrillard's theories see my "Pop's Public Relations: Pop Art 1955-70 by Henry Geldzahler," *Art & Text* 19, October-December 1985, pp. 82-87. In the seventies and eighties Baudrillard developed his concept of "Simulacrum" which he considers emblematically realized in Pop. See "Pop: An Art Of Consumption?" in this volume. For representative formulations of Baudrillard's "simul-acrum" see the collections, *For a Critique of the Political Economy of the Sign*, C. Levin, St. Louis, Missouri, 1981 and *Simulations*, trans. P. Foss, P. Patton and P. Beitchman, New York 1983. Baudrillard has become the most prolific and well-known of the theorists who have been informed by Marxist and linguistic theories and who have examined late capitalism as a society of consumption. For Baudrillard, late capitalism is an age of simulation, where meaning (representational form) and value (economic worth) are generated within the circulation of an artificial and arbitrary cultural code.

14) "Crazy Golden Slippers," *Life,* January 21, 1957, pp. 12-13.

15) G.R. Swenson, "What is Pop Art, Part II," *Art News,* February 1964, p. 64.

BEYOND THE VANISHING POINT OF ART
J E A N   B A U D R I L L A R D

I must confess that my own relationship to the domain of
art and aesthetics has always been somewhat clandestine,
intermittent, ambivalent. But if I am basically an iconoclast, it
is because I come from a moralist and metaphysical tradition,
namely a political and ideological one. This tradition has
always mistrusted art, and culture in general; it has mistrusted
the very distinction between nature and culture, and between
art and reality, as being too boringly obvious. So to rely on art
has always seemed to me to be too easy—an undercommit
ment. It is as though we should not be able to practice art, to
enter the enchanted field of form and appearances, until all the
problems have been solved. Yet in its ideal definition, art *is* the
solution.

At its most profound level, art is seduction. But not wish-
ing to get involved in a discussion of that now, I have written
about art in terms of simulation and simulacra, and have
argued a skeptical, critical and paradoxical position, a challenge
to both the naïve exercise of reality and the naïve exercise of
art. So what follows is oriented more towards the status of art
objects than the practice of art as such—this is probably the

best way to consider contemporary art without prejudicing its value. Besides, one can feel justified in speaking from an iconoclastic position by the fact that art itself has become iconoclastic.

The following references to the modern condition of art are only isolated ones: they extend from Charles Baudelaire and his reflections on modernity, to Walter Benjamin and his analysis of the artwork and its technological reproduction, to Marshall McLuhan and his electronic pragmatism of the image, and finally, to Andy Warhol's ultra-mediated practice of art—his "transcendental non-aesthetics," or the euthanasia of art by itself. The internal movement of art history escapes me, even though I can enjoy it as an amateur. What is attractive to me is the line of destiny taken by artistic forms during the modern and contemporary eras: not the history of art, but its destiny, especially as it relates directly to the global euthanasia of political, ideological, and even sexual forms in our society. Not being privy to the history of art, I make no critique of it—nor do I pronounce upon any individual performance or collective movement. I do not consider how a particular art or aesthetic value is produced.

The xerox-degree of culture

The game of differences, of artistic supply and demand, the fluctuation in judgments of value, the social differentiation of aesthetic pleasure, etc., are all part of the mechanism of culture, to be explored according to sociological or semiological methods. But that reveals only the logic of the production of the aesthetic values. More interesting to explore is the fact that the logic of the production of values (and of surplus-values) converges with the opposite process: that of the disappearance of art.

The more aesthetic values come into the marketplace, the less possibility is there for aesthetic judgment or pleasure. The logic of the disappearance of art is, precisely, inversely proportional to that of the production of culture. The "xerox-degree" of culture in a state of absolute proliferation corresponds to the zero-degree of art: one is the other's vanishing point, and absolute simulation. This logic was inaugurated by Hegel when he spoke of the "mania for disappearance," and of how art would henceforth be implicated in the process of its own disappearance—from this a direct line links Baudelaire to Andy Warhol, under the sign of "absolute merchandise."

Faced with the great conflict between the concept of the artwork and modern industrial society, Baudelaire invented the first radical solution. To vulgar, capitalist society, and the new alienation of art in terms of commercial value, Baudelaire opposed not a defense of the traditional status of the artwork, but a total objectivization of it: since aesthetic value risks being alienated by commercialization, it should not turn away from this alienation, but go further into it and fight it with its own weapons. It should follow the inexorable paths of indifference and commercial equivalence, and transform the work of art into absolute merchandise. Confronted by the challenge of modernity, art should not look for its salvation in nostalgic refusal, for then it becomes only art for art's sake, a futile and powerless mirror of capitalism and of the fatality of merchandise. Instead, it should reinforce the formal and fetishized abstraction of merchandise, the enchantment of exchange-value, by becoming more merchandise than merchandise itself: namely, by moving even further away from use-value, while escaping from exchange-value by radicalizing it. The absolute object is precisely that which has no value, has an indifferent quality, but which escapes objective alienation by becoming more object than object. This gives it a fatal quality.

This overthrow of exchange value, this destruction of merchandise through its own value, is visible in today's art market. The wild speculation on works of art is a parody of the market, an inherent derision of commercial value. The whole law of equivalence is broken, and we enter a sphere which is no longer that of value, but of the phantasm of value: the ecstasy of absolute value. This is relevant not only on an economic level, but on an aesthetic one as well. Here we are in the ecstatic state of value, that is, at the point where all aesthetic values (styles, manners, abstraction or figuration, the neo, the retro, etc.) are simultaneously, and potentially, at a maximum. Everything is on the hit parade at the same time, by special effect, and without any possibility of comparison or judgment of value. We are in the jungle of fetish-objects; and as we know, fetish objects have no value in themselves. Or rather, they only have value to the degree that they can no longer be exchanged.

So here lies the contemporary scene, in that very irony Baudelaire intended for the work of art: a supremely ironic merchandise, because it has no other—more arbitrary or even irrational—meaning than as merchandise, and so circulates ever more rapidly and assumes ever more value as it increasingly loses its meaning and its reference. Ultimately, Baudelaire was not far from putting the artwork on the same footing as fashion itself, under the triumphant sign of modernity. Fashion as ultramerchandise, and hence as both an apotheosis and a radical parody of this merchandise.

In *Stances* (Edition Christian Bourgeois) Giorgio Agamben says:

[*Baudelaire*] *approved the new character conferred on the object through its transformation into merchandise. He was conscious of the fatal power of attraction that this character brings to the artwork . . . The genius of Baudelaire was to confront the invasion of commercialization by transforming the artwork itself into merchandise and fetish . . . The aura of cold intangibility that then began to surround the artwork is the equivalent of the fetish character conferred on merchandise by its exchange-value . . .*

Baudelaire did not limit himself to reproducing the division between exchange-value and use-value in the artwork. He intended to create a merchandise of a certain absolute *type, in which the process of fetishization was to be taken to the very point of annihilating the merchandise's own reality. A merchandise whose use-value and exchange value mutually abolish each other is no longer merchandise.*

Thus the transformation of a work of art into absolute merchandise is also the most radical abolition of merchandise. *This is why Baudelaire places the experience of "shock" at the center of his artistic endeavor. "Shock" is the potential for strangeness that objects assume when, in order to put on the enigmatic mask of merchandise, they lose their authority as use-value . . . Baudelaire asserted that to ensure the survival of art in industrial civilization, the artist must try to reproduce in his work the destruction of use-value and traditional intelligibility... The self-negation of art therefore becomes its only possibility for survival.*

As Agamben goes on to say: "It is fortunate that the founder of modern poetry was a fetishist . . . Only a fetishist could emerge victorious in the confrontation with merchandise."

If the merchandise form shatters the object's past ideality (its beauty, its authenticity, and even its functionality), then we must not try to resuscitate it by denying the formal essence of merchandise. On the contrary—and here is the whole strategy, perhaps the very perversion and seduction of modernity for Baudelaire—we must push this partition of value to the absolute limit. There is no dialectic between the two, synthesis is a feeble solution; dialectics is always a nostalgic operation. The only radical and modern solution is to potentialize what is new, original, unexpected or inspired in merchandise: namely, the formal indifference to utility and value, with pre-eminence being given to unrestricted circulation. That is what the work of art must accomplish: to assume all the characteristics of shock, strangeness, surprise, disturbance, liquidity, and even the self-destruction, instantaneousness and hyper-reality of merchandise.

It must exponentialize the inhumanity of exchange-value in a sort of erotic ecstasy, but also with an ironic indifference to the paths of alienation. That is why, in the enchanted/ironic (and non-dialectical) logic of Baudelaire, the artwork converges with fashion, advertising, with the whole "enchantment of the code," glistening in all its venality, its mobility, its non-referential effects, its aleatory and vertiginous qualities—a pure object of magical interchangeability, since, causes having disappeared, all effects are virtually equivalent.

The effects can also be nil, as we well know. But it is up to the artwork to fetishize this nothingness, this disappearance, and to derive extraordinary effects from it. This new form of seduction is no longer that of mastering conventional effects (the mastery of illusion and the aesthetic order), but rather that of the vertigo of obscenity. Yet who can say there is any difference? Vulgar merchandise only generates a universe of production—and God knows if this universe is melancholic! Raised to the power of absolute merchandise, it produces effects of seduction.

The art object, as the new triumphant fetish (and not a sad, alienated fetish), must work of itself to deconstruct its traditional aura, its authority and its power of illusion, in order to glow in the pure obscenity of merchandise. It must disappear as a familiar object, and become *monstrously strange*. But this strangeness is no longer the disquietude of the repressed or alienated object, this object does not glow with an obsession or secret dispossession. It glows because it has exceeded its own form to become a pure object, a pure event.

This perspective, inspired in Baudelaire by the spectacle of the transfiguration of merchandise in the World Exposition of 1855, is superior in a number of points to that of Walter Benjamin. In "The Work of Art in the Age of Mechanical Reproduction" Benjamin derives, from the object's diminishing aura and authenticity, a desperately political (i.e., politically despairing) conclusion that ushers in a melancholic modernity; whereas Baudelaire's position is infinitely more modern (but perhaps it was only possible to be truly modern in the 19th century). Baudelaire argued for the exploration of new forms of seduction, linked to pure objects, to pure events, to that modern passion which is fascination, and so was better able to resist that depressing theory of alienation (which, besides, has had such a devastating effect on the poverty of 20th century thought). Possibly due to the historical novelty of the emergence of merchandise, he better understood what was the only genuine aesthetic and metaphysical response to this challenge. And it isn't necessary here to refer to Baudelaire's own "aesthetic" preoccupation. His idea of absolute merchandise sheds new light on all fields of analysis.

When Andy Warhol undertook that radical attempt to become an absolute "machine," to become more machine than a machine, by the automatic, mechanical reproduction of objects already mechanical, already manufactured (whether a soup can or a star's face), he linked up with Baudelaire's idea of absolute merchandise and brought to perfection his vision of the destiny of modern art, even while trying to escape from it—by taking it through to the end, that is say, to the very denial of itself in a negative ecstasy of value and also of representation. If, as Baudelaire said, the modern artist's vocation is to give merchandise a heroic status, whereas the bourgeoisie only give it a sentimental expression in advertising. This means that heroism does not at all consist in the resanctification of art and value in opposition to merchandise (that would indeed be sentimental, though it is still the standard impulse today), but in the sanctification of merchandise as merchandise, which would tend to make Warhol the hero, or the anti-hero, of modern art, since it was he who pushed to the furthest the ritual paths of art's disappearance, of all sentimentality in art, its ritual of negative transparency and radical indifference to its own authenticity. The modern hero no longer incarnates the sublime in art, but the objective irony of the world of merchandise. He is the ironic hero of art's disappearance.

But this disappearance is not negative or depressing—no more than merchandise is. In the mind of Baudelaire, it is an object of enthusiasm: there is a modern enchantment of merchandise, just as there is an enchantment in the disappearance of art. Of course, it is a matter of knowing how to disappear. The whole disappearance of art, hence its modernity, is the art of disappearance. This is its difference from conventional, triumphalist art of the 19th and 20th centuries: official art, art for art's sake, etc., the art born at the very time of Baudelaire, and which he detested as such—and which is far from dead, since it is triumphantly rehabilitated in today's international museums. The whole difference between this art and the other is in the secret abnegation of its own disappearance (abnegation is a heroic virtue, a choice made almost unconsciously by authentic art). By contrast, official art doesn't want to disappear. It doesn't put its own existence at stake — and just for that it disappeared from our minds for a century. Its triumphant reappearance today, in the postmodern era, suggests that the great modern adventure of art's disappearance is finished.

In Warhol, the decision to disappear is made almost too consciously, too cynically, but it is no less a heroic choice. His art is cool, even though the art of disappearance can take either a hot or a cool form. Yet it still ends in a kind of fatality, that is to say, an end without finality—in contrast to Kant's finality without end, which characterizes a classical aesthetics or ethics. In this nebulous, explosive as well as implosive, state of modern art, a double spiral of hot and cool should be traced, similar to what can occur in the sphere of the media (according to McLuhan's distinction) or in the sphere of war, in the alternation between hot and cold war. Art is not separable from everything else, particularly the media and war. If one could take a global view of things, one would find everywhere, in art as in the media and war, the actual supremacy of cold forms.

We must bear a fatal strategy in mind, the final explosion of hot art, of hot painting in the frozen time of cold war, for art is never the mechanical reflection of positive or negative conditions in the world. It is the exaggerated illusion of it, its hyperbolic mirror. Abstract expressionism, the "hot" painting of the era, is not only the reflection of the immanent and suspended global nuclear conflict. While this catastrophe, this final event does not actually happen, art goes further; it brings this menace into effect, it anticipates this form of extermination in a symbolic gesture. Art doesn't try to escape the catastrophe through an idealistic figuration; it goes right to the end, exterminating itself and giving all the signs of its own disappearance as art. In this way, it challenges the extermination of the world.

Art has no critical meaning and offers no dialectical solution. It *is* the solution by its own action. It challenges the world by exceeding it; it resolves it by overtaking, overwhelming, exorcising and symbolically deterring it. To a full and saturated system (of production or destruction, of objects or signs) it opposes the inverse or homologous aspect of a pure, empty gesture. This is its fatal strategy, its mania for signifying nothing, its mania for signifying even when there is no longer any meaning to be given or alternative to be found. To force the real, to force appearances even by its own disappearance—art has never done anything else. It summons the real to vanish, and thus introduces, in defiance of the normal course of world events, the conditions of the Last Judgment.

Unlike classical art, modern art does not exercise the symbolic mastery of presence and transcendence: it exercises only the symbolic mastery of disappearance. And its charm is no longer that of the seduction of forms, as in classical art; it is the magic of its own disappearance. It is a fascination, not seduction. Don't be fooled! Life is no longer to be found in the aesthetic dimension of the gaze, but in the tactile vertigo of the image, in its vertiginous absorption, exactly like the world that surrounds us. Art no longer has a link with history and continuity, but is caught in a chain reaction, that of simulacra and simulation, which is exactly parallel and isomorphous with the potential nuclear chain reaction. The chain reaction of Hiroshima put an end to history. The chain reaction of simulacra put an end to art.

Hot painting, abstract expressionism, illuminated the whole situation in a paradoxical way. It reflected a chain reaction of gestures, materials and colors, a sort of nuclear fusion of representation and form, and at the same time protested the involution of war into cold war, of the world into a cold world: the implosion of imagination into cool images and cool media. It was the last outburst, a final effort to reverse—even if it might be fatal to painting itself—the implacable process of deintensification. Hot painting was the last moment of *illuminated* art in a context of *non-illuminated* history, just before painting turned cool, frigid, in its Pop, photorealist and conceptual versions.

After the orgy

If I had to characterize this new state of affairs, I would call it "after the orgy." The orgy is in a way the whole explosive movement of modernity, with its various kinds of liberation—political liberation, sexual liberation, the liberation of productive and destructive forces, women's liberation, children's liberation, the liberation of unconscious drives, the liberation of art—the assumption of all models of representation, of all models of anti-representation. It is a total orgy: of the real, of the rational, of the sexual, of the critical and the anti-critical, of expansion and the crisis of expansion. We have exhausted all means of the production and virtual overproduction of objects, signs, messages, ideologies, pleasure. If you want my opinion, today everything is liberated. The game is over, and we collectively confront the crucial question: "What are you doing after the orgy?"

All we can do now is simulate the orgy and liberation, pretending to accelerate our move in this direction. But in reality we accelerate in a vacuum, because all the finalities of liberation (of production, of progress, of revolution) are already behind us: what we are haunted, or even obsessed by, is the anticipation of all the results, the availability of all the signs, of all the forms, of all desires, since everything has already been liberated. What happens then? A state of simulation, in which we can only replay all the scenarios because they have already taken place, either really or virtually. A state of realized utopia, of all realized utopias, where we must paradoxically live as if they were still to be realized. But since they are, and since we no longer have any hope of realizing them, all we can do is hyperrealize them in an indefinite simulation. We live in the indefinite reproduction of ideas, phantasms, images, dreams long since behind us, and yet which we must reproduce in a sort of fatal indifference.

This is true for all the domains: the great utopia of the social is realized through bureaucratic and totalitarian materialization of welfare. The great utopia of sex is realized through the technological, athletic and neurotic materialization of sexual practices. And the great utopia of art, the grand illusion, the revered transcendence of art, that too is materialized everywhere. People have argued that art has been dematerialized, but it is quite the contrary. Today art is to be found everywhere—in museums, in galleries, but also in debris, on walls, in the streets, in the banality of everything that is sanctified by the process of art. The aestheticization of the world is total.

Just as there is a bureaucratic materialization of the social, a technological materialization of the sexual, and a materialization in the media and advertising of the political, there is also a semiotic materialization of art. This is culture, understood as the circulation of signs. People complain about the commercialism of art, about the merchandizing of aesthetic values—but this is just a revival of the old bourgeois, nostalgic story. One should be much less afraid of commercial speculation than of the transcription of the whole environment into cultural and aesthetic terms, into museographic signs. But this is now our dominant culture—an immense enterprise of museographic reproduction, of aesthetic stockpiling, of resimulation and visual synthesizing of all the forms that surround us. That is the most serious menace, the "xerox-degree of culture."

With this present state of affairs, we are directly involved in giving an aesthetic and sentimental form to the world as it is—exactly the opposite of the heroic role of art that Baudelaire envisaged for the universe of merchandise and advertising which he detested so much. And this is what art has largely become: a prosthesis, just like culture in general. In place of the triumphant simulation imagined by Baudelaire we now have a depressing, repetitive simulation. Art has always been a simulacrum, but one which had the power of illusion. Our simulation is quite different, it relies solely on the sentimental vertigo of models. Art was once a dramatic simulacrum where illusion and reality played an antagonistic game. Now it is only an aesthetic prosthesis.

I have said that the sublime in modern art lies in the magic of its disappearance. But here the main danger for art comes from the *continuous replay* of this disappearance: all the forms of heroic disappearance, of the heroic abnegation of forms, of colors, of the very substance of art, have now unfolded as far as they can go, taking us to second- and third-degree forms of simulation (or whatever you like). We are in that perverse situation where not only has the utopia of art passed into reality (along with the utopias of the social, the political and the sexual), but also the very utopia of its disappearance, to which art is now dedicated to simulating. Thus each day we relive the disappearance of art in the repetition of its various forms (abstract or figurative, it doesn't matter), just as we relive the disappearance of political forms through their repetition in the media, or the disappearance of sexual forms through pornographic repetition in advertising.

Still, we should distinguish between those moments when

art retraces and celebrates its own disappearance—its phase of heroic simulation, one could say—and the occasions on which it treats this disappearance as a sort of negative heritage. The former is an original moment, occurring only once, even if it endures across the decades; while the latter can last for several centuries, but is no longer original. I belive that we are presently caught in this obsolete disappearance, in this outdated simulation, as one speaks of a "prolonged" coma.

The illuminating moment for art is its own loss. There is the illuminating moment of simulation, of sacrifice almost, where art is immersed in banality (Heidegger correctly said that the fall into banality was the second fall of man, his modern destiny). But the non-illuminating moment of art is when it learns to survive this very banality, somewhat like failing at suicide. To succeed at suicide is the art of disappearance, namely, to give to this disappearance all the prestige of artifice. Yet many who fail at suicide do not fail to achieve glory and success. As we know, failing at suicide is often the best form of publicity.

In brief, to take up Benjamin's notion of the aura of authenticity and of the original, there is also an aura of the simulacrum, of simulation. I would even dare to say that there is authentic as well as inauthentic simulation, "true" as well as "false" simulation, however paradoxical that might seem. When Warhol painted Campbell's Soup cans in the sixties, it was a brilliant gesture of simulation for all of modern art: at one and the same time, both object-merchandise and sign-merchandise found themselves ironically sanctified—which is the only ritual left to us, that of transparency. But when he painted his Campbell Soup boxes in 1986, he was no longer

185

making an innovation, he was acting out a sterotype of simulation. In 1965 he attacked the concept of originality in an original way; in 1986, he reproduced the unoriginal in an unoriginal way. In 1965, a whole aesthetic trauma had occurred over the irruption of merchandise in art, which was treated in an ascetic as well as ironic way (reflecting an asceticism of merchandise that was both puritan and magical—"enigmatic," Marx said), and which simplified artistic practice in a single blow. The geniality of merchandise, the evil genie of merchandise evoked a new geniality in art: the genie of simulation. Nothing of that remains in 1986, however; only the genie of advertising can illustrate this new phase of merchandise. Again, it is official art alone which aestheticizes merchandise, where once more one encounters that sentimentality stigmatized by Baudelaire.

You will perhaps reply that redoing the same thing after twenty years is an even more extreme irony. I don't think so. I believe in the genie of simulation, not in its phantom. Nor in its cadaver, even in stereo. I know that in a few centuries there won't be any difference between a genuine Pompeian villa and the Paul Getty Museum in Malibu, between the French Revolution and its commemoration in the 1984 Los Angeles Olympics—but *we* still live in this difference and derive our energy from it. I am not saying that there isn't a vertigo, a fascination in total indifference, in the total confusion between forms and their double: but as for us, it seems to me that it is not impossible to tell the difference.

The whole dilemma is there. Either simulation is irreversible—there is nothing beyond simulation, it is no longer even an event, it is our absolute banality, our everyday

186

obscenity, we are in a stage of permanent nihilism, and we are facing a senseless repetition of all the forms of our culture, while waiting for another unpredictable event (but where would it come from?)— or else there is still an art of simulation, an ironic quality which constantly resuscitates the appearances of the world in order to destroy them. Otherwise as is often the case today, art would only be pursued by its own cadaver. You don't have to add the same to the same, to infinity—that is a poor form of simulation. One should separate the same from the same. Each image should deprive the world of reality; in each image the temptation of total destruction, of permanent entropy: the form of disappearance should be lively, which is the secret of art and of seduction. There is in all art, in classical just as much as contemporary art, a double postulation, and hence a double strategy—a drive to destruction, to efface every trace of the world and reality, and, on the other hand, a resistance to this drive. As Henri Michaux said: "The artist is the person who resists with all his energy the fundamental drive to leave no trace."

I have said that I am an iconoclast, and that art itself has become iconoclastic. By this I mean the new modern form of iconoclasm, which does not consist of destroying images but of manufacturing images, a profusion of images *in which there is nothing to see.* These are, literally, images which leave no trace. They are without aesthetic qualities as such—except for the professionals in the art world. But, behind each of the images, something has disappeared. That is their secret, if they have one—and that is also the secret of simulation, if it has one.

Now, upon reflection, that was the very problem of Iconoclasm in Byzantine times. The Iconolaters were discerning people who pretended to represent God to his greater glory, but who in reality, by simulating God in images, dissimulated as a consequence the very question of his existence. Each image was a pretext for not posing the question of God's existence. Behind each image, in fact, God had disappeared. He wasn't dead, he had disappeared; that is to say, the question of his existence was no longer even posed. The question of God's existence or non-existence was resolved through simulation.

But it is possible to think that this was God's own strategy for disappearing, and precisely behind images. God himself makes use of images in order to disappear, by obeying the fundamental drive not to leave any trace. Thus the prophecy is fulfilled: we live in a world of simulation, in a world where the highest function of the sign is to make reality disappear, and at the same time to mask this disappearance. Isn't this what art does? Certainly, the media do little else today. This is why they pursue the same destiny.

But we can assume another hypothesis. Suppose that the aesthetic era, the age of art and artworks, was born out of the desanctification of the former religious world and its rituals; suppose that the artwork succeeded the ritual object in a sort of iconic genealogy; suppose that this age of art is now over, since art can do nothing but repeat its own simulation. Why shouldn't we assume that another mutation of the same kind could happen?

Originally the fetish was not considered beautiful. It became beautiful when it lost the supernatural intensity of religious immanence. Today, the artwork can't be called beautiful anymore; it has lost its aesthetic intensity and its quality as art. Perhaps art has only been a short parenthesis in human history, exploited since the Renaissance and now already dead, as the immanence of objects, images and media has been substituted for transcendence.

Art is our new fetish. But perhaps it is also the beginning of a new race or species of objects, as radically new compared to art as art was compared to the sacred. From now on we will live in a world without originals, as it was for objects and images before art existed. And in the absence of originality we may recover some of these ritual forms, but certainly they will not be the same as those existing before the age of aesthetics. Our forms and images are beyond aesthetics, just as our media are beyond the true and the false, and our values are beyond good and evil. But there is always a point beyond the vanishing point. There is always a time after the orgy. A secret reversibility lies in all things, even when they seem to be irreversible. Reversibility is beautiful.

So if we again ask the question of what to do after the orgy of modernism, then the answer lies, I believe, in the perpetual reversal, in their new ironic beginning of things, as in precisely that story when, during an orgy, someone whispers in another's ear: "What are you doing after the orgy?"

NEW CRITICISM
Series